Reminiscences of

Captain Charles Henry Kretz, Jr.

Supply Corps, U.S. Navy (Retired)

U.S. Naval Institute

Annapolis, Maryland

1986

Preface

The Asiatic Fleet, which for many years represented U.S. national interests in China, now exists only in memory. In that fleet of the pre-World War II years, there grew up a breed of officers and enlisted men known as old China hands. Though officially part of the U.S. Navy, they necessarily developed a number of practices and ways of life which were distinctly different from those in the U.S. Fleet which operated off the coasts of the United States. In this memoir, one of the old China hands recalls what it was like to serve in the USS Panay and the USS Bulmer in the late 1930s, shortly before the U.S. entrance into World War II. From the vantage point of a then-junior officer, Captain Kretz was a firsthand observer of the Sino-Japanese War which started more than four years before the United States was brought into the conflict by the attack on Pearl Harbor. Combining that perspective with his recollections of the Chinese culture provides a fascinating memoir of a time now past.

The interviews with Captain Kretz were conducted for the Naval Institute by Captain Paul B. Ryan, USN (Ret.). The volume was indexed by Ms. Susan Sweeney; the transcribing and smooth typing were done by Mrs. Deborah Reid. Prior to his death, Captain Kretz had the opportunity to make changes and corrections to the transcript. Some additional editing was done as part of the process of putting the transcript into smooth form. That editing meant deletion of some unnecessary material but nothing of substance. The original transcript containing Captain Kretz's handwritten corrections is on file at the Naval Institute.

                                                              Paul Stillwell
                                                              Director of Oral History
                                                              U.S. Naval Institute
                                                              December 1986

CAPTAIN CHARLES HENRY KRETZ, JR.
SUPPLY CORPS, U. S. NAVY (RETIRED)

Charles Henry Kretz, Jr., was born on 17 February 1910, in Beaumont, Texas, son of the late Charles H. and Elizabeth McCormick Kretz. He was graduated from St. Mary's, Kansas, High School in 1927 and attended St. Mary's College for a year before entering the U.S. Naval Academy, Annapolis, Maryland, in 1928. As a midshipman he was crew coxswain, a member of the rifle team, and business manager of "Reef Points." Graduated and commissioned ensign on 2 June 1932, he subsequently attained the rank of captain, to date from 1 July 1951.

Upon graduation from the Naval Academy in June 1932, he was assigned to the USS Arkansas (BB-33), and two years later was transferred to the USS Idaho (BB-42). In February 1936 he reported to Asiatic Station, where he had successive duty, until September 1938, in the USS Panay (PR-5) and the USS Bulmer (DD-222), being attached to the latter during the Sino-Japanese War. From October 1938 until July of the following year he served in the USS Wasmuth (DD-338), a unit of Destroyers, Battle Force.

He was personnel officer at the Naval Air Station, Pensacola, Florida, from July 1939 until March 1941, and when the United States entered World War II in December 1941, he was at sea as executive officer of the USS Williamson (AVD-2). The Williamson operated, during the first months of the war, in support of Patrol Wing Four in the Aleutians, and on convoy and escort duty. Detached in February 1942, he was ordered to the USS Indiana (BB-58), then being fitted out at the Newport News Shipbuilding and Dry Dock Company, Newport News, Virginia. He served aboard that battleship from her commissioning, 30 April 1942, until September 1943, during which period she operated in the Pacific, in support of the Rennell Island operation; as a part of Task Group 36.3 in the New Georgia campaign; and with Task Force 58 in the Marcus Island raid.

For four months in 1943 he was an instructor in the Naval Reserve Officers Training Corps unit of the University of Southern California, and from January 1944 until March 1945 served in the Bureau of Naval Personnel, Navy Department, Washington, D.C. Transferring from the line to the Supply Corps of the Navy in March 1945, he attended the Supply Corps School, Harvard University, and after the cessation of hostilities, served as supply officer of the USS Washington (BB-56) from September 1945 to April 1946. He then had similar duty for a year in the USS New Jersey (BB-62).

Duty as assistant supply officer of the USS Wasp (CV-18) from April 1947 until May 1949, was followed by duty as supply and finance officer of the U.S. Marine Corps Air Station, El Toro, California. In July 1950 he returned to the Navy Department for duty in the Fiscal Division of the Bureau of Aeronautics.

Subsequent tours of duty included service as supply officer of the Cherry Point Marine Corps Air Station, duty on the staff of the Commandant of the 12th Naval District, and command of the Naval Supply Center, Pearl Harbor, Hawaii. He retired from active duty in 1957.

Captain Kretz was married to the former Audrey Raymer of Los Angeles, California. They had two sons and seven grandchildren. Captain Kretz died 30 January 1986 at Sequoia Hospital, Redwood City, California.

Authorization

The U.S. Naval Institute is hereby authorized to make available to individuals, libraries and other repositories of its choosing the transcripts of three oral history interviews concerning the naval service of the late Captain Charles Henry Kretz, Jr. U.S. Navy (Retired). These three interviews were recorded on 27 March 1984, 3 April 1984, and 11 April 1984 by Captain Kretz and the undersigned in collaboration with Captain Paul B. Ryan, U.S. Navy (Retired), who was representing the U.S. Naval Institute.

The undersigned does hereby release and assign to the U.S. Naval Institute all right, title, restrictions, and interest in the interviews. The copyright in both the oral and transcribed versions shall be the sole property of the U.S. Naval Institute. The tape recordings of the interviews are and will remain the property of the U.S. Naval Institute.

Signed and sealed this _Sixth_ day of ~~December 1986.~~ January 1987

Mrs. Audrey R. Kretz

Interview Number 1 with Captain Charles Henry Kretz, Jr.,
U.S. Navy (Retired)

Place: Captain Kretz's home in San Mateo, California

Date: 27 March 1984

Subject: U.S. Asiatic Fleet

Interviewer: Captain Paul B. Ryan, U.S. Navy (Retired)

Q: Captain Kretz is an old Yangtze Patrol sailor. We will talk about his days in the 1930s aboard ships in the Yang Pat. Captain, before we start, suppose you tell something of yourself and your Naval Academy class and your duty before you went to China.

Captain Kretz: I entered the Naval Academy in 1928, and after four years, I graduated from the Naval Academy. My first assignment was in the battleship Arkansas, which was based at that time at Long Beach, California. She had on board a contingent of Marines that we were supposed to take to Korea, due to the Japanese involvement in Korea at that time. We stood by for many months in Long Beach but were never actually ordered to Korea. Finally, the Marines were removed from the ship, and we got back a regular crew of sailors to man the ship.

That summer, we made a cruise in the Arkansas with the ROTC from the University of California and the University of Washington to the Hawaiian Islands, and then returned to Long

Kretz #1 - 2

Beach, where we joined the fleet.*

Q: This is 1933?

Captain Kretz: 1933. In July of 1934, I was ordered to the Idaho, and in March of 1936, I was ordered to the Asiatic Fleet. Upon arrival in China, I was assigned to the Yangtze Patrol, USS Panay, which at that time was based in I-ch'ang, which is right at the mouth of the gorges of the Yangtze River.

Q: Captain, when you were detached from the Idaho in Long Beach, I presume that you were ordered to San Francisco for transportation. Were you married at the time?

Captain Kretz: Yes, I was married. We proceeded to China via the SS President Hayes. That was a President Lines ship.

Q: I suppose that this was a really nice occasion for you to have a vacation.

Captain Kretz: And we really did. We really enjoyed the whole trip.

---

*ROTC--Reserve Officer Training Corps. Summer cruises were customary for NROTC midshipmen, just as they were for midshipmen from the Naval Academy.

Kretz #1 - 3

Q: Can you tell us something about the activities on board?

Captain Kretz: Well, during the trip, we had all sorts of shipboard activities such as playing shuffleboard, ping-pong, and table golf. We had a table by ourselves until we reached San Francisco. Actually, we had joined the ship in Long Beach and took her to San Francisco, where she picked up the remainder of her passengers to China.

Q: How was the weather?

Captain Kretz: The weather was great, but it rained, and I'll describe what my wife said about the rain: "It just rained hard like a brief flash of lightning. It's superb. Nothing but a blue-gray sea and rain like silver arrows. The whole world, as far as I could see, was water and nothing but water. Even the air was filled with it, and in a brief instant was gone."

Q: I take it that you're reading, Captain, excerpts of letters that Mrs. Kretz wrote back in 1936 to a friend of hers back home, which now are preserved, and so we have it actually as it was.

Captain Kretz: That is correct, we do.

Q: On board these ships going to China, you had people, I

presume, who were not only service people--Army, Navy--but you had Standard Oil people, commercial bankers headed for Shanghai, and missionaries. Is that the sort of passengers you had?

Captain Kretz: We had passengers, but very few. We had one passenger with his family, who had served as a civilian with Admiral Peary in the North Pole.*

Q: That was in 1909.

Captain Kretz: Yes. He was on board, and we had a few other passengers. I don't remember too much about them, because the Navy passengers more or less stayed together during the trip. But we were congenial with the other people.

Q: Do you recall any of your naval colleagues on the voyage with you?

Captain Kretz: Yes, Lieutenant Steinbauer.**

Q: What class was he?

**Commander Robert E. Peary, USN, is widely credited with being the first man to reach the North Pole, achieving that feat in April 1909. There are, however, a number of people who contest his claim. For more on the subject, see Commander Edward P. Stafford, USN(Ret.), "Peary and the North Pole: Not the Shadow of a Doubt," U.S. Naval Institute Proceedings, December 1971, pages 44-55.

**Lieutenant Frederick S. Steinbauer, USN.

Captain Kretz: He was in the class of '21. He was also ordered to the Panay, as the executive officer. And later we traveled up the Yangtze River together, to the Panay. The other things that we had on board the President Hayes going out were concerts at dinner every night, bingo, dancing, horse racing, Monopoly, and movies every night--very elegant.

Q: Captain, what was the itinerary of the President Hayes after you left San Francisco?

Captain Kretz: Our first stop, of course, was Honolulu. From Honolulu, we proceeded directly to Kobe, and from Kobe to Shanghai.

Q: Then you reported to the senior officer in Shanghai for your orders, I presume.

Captain Kretz: I reported to the senior officer on what we called then the "outside gunboat." I think it was the Tulsa, but I'm not sure. But most of the paperwork at that time was handled by what we referred to as NavPur, which was the Navy Purchasing Office, located ashore in Shanghai.

Q: It was a shore administration office.

Captain Kretz: Yes, shore administration office, and they handled all sorts of things for Navy personnel all over the China station.

Q: Was this NavPur office also a godsend for young Navy wives, helping them to get located?

Captain Kretz: It sure was.

Q: Perhaps you can tell us where you found living quarters.

Captain Kretz: We found living quarters in the Palace Hotel, which was right off of the Bund, almost on the Bund in Shanghai.*

Q: Was it a hotel room with a kitchenette?

Captain Kretz: Yes, it was a hotel room. Of course, we had our meals in the hotel restaurant.

Q: What did you pay for the room? Do you recall the amount?

Captain Kretz: It was very little. I don't remember the amount, but the exchange at that time was 3.5 to 1--Chinese dollars to

---

*The Bund is a noted thoroughfare which runs along the waterfront of the Whangpoo River.

one American dollar. And you could buy about as much for one Chinese dollar as you could with one American dollar in the United States.

Q: So as a j.g., you were making something in the order of maybe not quite $200 a month?* $210, maybe?

Captain Kretz: $271.

Q: $271 with living quarters?

Captain Kretz: With living quarters, yes.

Q: And you got $60 a month for living quarters?

Captain Kretz: Yes, yes. The whole thing was $271.

Q: And then you got $82, so you each got $41 ration, I think. And so it added up to a lot of money in China.

Captain Kretz: It did. I hadn't drawn pay for, I guess, about six weeks, and I went down to the station gunboat and drew my pay. I was paid in Chinese $10 bills which were stacked ten to a

---

*j.g.--lieutenant (junior grade).

package, and I could hardly carry all the packages back up to the hotel room.

Q: Did you use rickshaws as transportation all the way?

Captain Kretz: Yes, we always used rickshaws.

Q: Did Mrs. Kretz become accustomed to the shopping and Shanghai life?

Captain Kretz: Very much so.

Mrs. Kretz: Very quickly.

Q: And I presume that there was a Navy colony there so that the wives helped each other in getting oriented and so forth?

Captain Kretz: Well, at that time, we were only there for a few days before we left to go up the river on a British riverboat, to go up to I-ch'ang to join the Panay.

Q: Captain, do you have any recollections of your first trip up the Yangtze?

Captain Kretz: Yes, quite a few, I think. One of the first

things that we realized was every town that we stopped in along the river--and I think we stopped in all of them--all the foreigners knew us and knew all about us. It was just like a small town 1,500 miles long.

Q: What do you attribute this to?

Captain Kretz: I guess it's the bamboo communication system in China, which is fantastic. I'll tell you how I found out through the same system that I had a son born, but that will come later in the interview.

One thing that really impressed us was on Easter Sunday in 1936. We were aboard the British ship SS Wulin, a river passenger ship and cargo ship, and we stopped in Wuhu.* My wife and I went ashore, took a walk around the town, and during that walk we passed a Chinese cemetery. Of course, in those days, when you went ashore in China, you always carried a cane, mainly to beat off the dogs. As we passed this cemetery, there were a lot of dogs rooting around in the graves. The Chinese do not bury their people; they just put the coffins on top of the ground and go off and leave them, unless they're very wealthy, and then they may cover them with a little dirt. Well, these dogs were actually rooting in the coffins. That wasn't a very pleasant

---

*The Wulin was a 2,515-ton, 249-foot-long river steamer operated by the China Navigation Company, Ltd.

Easter Sunday for us.

Q: Did you have a nice dining room and staterooms?

Captain Kretz: Yes, yes. We had good food.

Q: Do you recall the river as clean or dirty?

Captain Kretz: Dirty. Very dirty.

Q: Was the scenery spectacular?

Captain Kretz: The scenery was absolutely different. Some of it was spectacular, yes, but a lot of it was just looking out over the plains and the farmers and their little farmhouses. But every once in a while, something would appear, like a huge rock a couple of hundred feet high in the river with a pagoda sitting on top of it.

Q: So they chose well their locations for temples.

Captain Kretz: Yes, they did.

Q: What kind of quarters did you find in I-ch'ang for your wife?

Kretz #1 - 11

Captain Kretz: Well, when we arrived in I-ch'ang, we found that the Standard Oil people had given the American naval officers a house, which was quite large and modern, with modern sanitation, which was an unheard of thing in the interior of China.

Q: It had bathrooms, you mean?

Captain Kretz: Yes, yes.

Mrs. Kretz: And running water.

Captain Kretz: We had a reception hall, living room, club room, a kitchen, a servants' quarters. Upstairs there were three bedrooms and two baths, a dining room, and a veranda. Also a pretty garden and a miniature golf and tennis court. That constituted the compound. The installation, of course, contained tanks and so forth, and it was all guarded, extra military guards, particularly when Admiral Murfin came up, with walls and sentries and dogs.*

Q: You mention Admiral Murfin. He was Commander in Chief Asiatic Fleet.

---

*Admiral Orin G. Murfin, USN, served as Commander in Chief U.S. Asiatic Fleet from 4 October 1935 to 30 October 1936. His flagship was the USS Augusta (CA-31).

Captain Kretz: Yes, while we were there he made a trip up with his wife and daughter.

Q: Did you live ashore while the ship was anchored there?

Captain Kretz: Yes. When I didn't have the duty, I lived ashore.

Q: And I know that everybody who went to China speaks of the marvelous servants that they had. Did you enjoy this privilege too?

Captain Kretz: We sure did. I'll read this to you. My wife says, "I have a number one boy, amah, innumerable boys. When I enter the kitchen, they all stand at attention and salute, saying, 'Good morning, sir.' I remember ordering a peanut butter sandwich and being brought two pieces of bread, buttered, with whole peanuts spread inside."

Q: So there was a culture shock there. When did you find the Panay?

Captain Kretz: I found the Panay; she was moored to a pontoon in I-ch'ang when the Wulin arrived. The skipper's name was Chester

Holton.*

Q: And the executive officer, you've already mentioned.

Captain Kretz: That was Steinbauer.

Q: How many officers were aboard?

Captain Kretz: We had the captain, Steinbauer, myself, and Phil Mothersill, who was the chief engineer.** That was it, as far as officers were concerned, besides a doctor. We had a doctor on board.***

Q: It took you, what, a week to get to I-ch'ang from Shanghai? How far were you, 1,000 miles?

Captain Kretz: About 1,000 miles, yes. It took better than a week because we stopped at every port.

Q: I see. Were there other foreign gunboats there at I-ch'ang also?

---
*Lieutenant Commander Chester M. Holton, USN.
**Lieutenant (junior grade) Philip W. Mothersill, Jr., USN.
***The doctor was Lieutenant (junior grade) Cecil D. Riggs, Medical Corps, USN.

Kretz #1 - 14

Captain Kretz: Yes, there were several Japanese gunboats at I-ch'ang.

Q: As a young officer, did you and your colleagues have any deep conception of why we had an American naval presence in China?

Captain Kretz: Oh, yes, we certainly did.

Q: How would you recollect this?

Captain Kretz: Well, one of the things was that we had missionaries. I'm talking about the Yangtze River now. We had missionaries all along the Yangtze River, and they were constantly being attacked and kidnapped by the various warlords or bandits.

Q: Yes, both, I'd say.

Captain Kretz: And then held for ransom. In fact, we stopped at one town, I've forgotten what town it was, but I think it was Kukiang, and the captain of the Wulin had two American nuns aboard who had just been released from being captured.

As I remember, at that time, the guns aboard the Panay had been fired more times in action, repelling the Chinese pirates, than they had in practice.

Kretz #1 - 15

Q: Did you have two 3-inch guns?

Captain Kretz: Two 3-inch, yes.

Q: Plus .50-caliber machine guns, probably.

Captain Kretz: Plus .30-caliber machine guns. The 3-inch guns were manually trained and manually elevated.

Q: So you were very much aware of the need for the American naval presence, and the Standard Oil people were certainly happy to have you there.

Captain Kretz: That's right. Yes.

Q: Captain, when you went aboard, did you find yourself to be the junior officer and get all the odd jobs on board ship?

Captain Kretz: I got all the odd jobs and then some. My principal assignment was communication officer and assistant first lieutenant. But anything that came along would be my job to do, generally.

Q: What kind of accommodations on board were there?

Kretz #1 - 16

Captain Kretz: We had nice staterooms. They weren't large but they were very comfortable.

Q: Two men to a room?

Captain Kretz: One man to a room. We had a small wardroom, but it was adequate. On the upper deck, under an awning, we had what we called a "Palm Garden," where we had movies and a place up there during time off, going up and down the river. Our mess boys were Chinese, and they were semiofficial Navy personnel. They did not actually belong to the United States Navy, but they were paid by the Navy.

Q: And they were recruited for that cruise.

Captain Kretz: For that ship.

Q: And they stayed on board and never left China?

Captain Kretz: No, they stayed on that ship, and the ones we had were very good. But then you asked about the others--most of the sailors had their own boys to do their own work, so they just told the boys what to do, and the Chinese did the work.

Q: What kind of morale did you have on board the ship among the

Kretz #1 - 17

American crew?

Captain Kretz: I thought we had excellent morale.

Q: Do you think it took a special type of sailor to be a China sailor?

Captain Kretz: Yes and no. Some were and some were not. I don't want to go into that in more detail.

Q: Captain, you mentioned the name of the skipper was Lieutenant Commander Holton, and the exec was Lieutenant Steinbauer.

Captain Kretz: The other line officer was Phil Mothersill. And the other officer was the doctor, who was Cecil Riggs, who later became Inspector General of the Medical Corps of the Navy.

Q: And how were the relations of the officers with the captain?

Captain Kretz: They were horrible, frankly.

Q: Was he eccentric?

Captain Kretz: Very eccentric.

Kretz #1 - 18

Q: Do you want to elaborate on that?

Captain Kretz: Yes, I'll elaborate on it. I'll tell you a specific instance. He came aboard with the illusion that he and his wife had been followed by a pair of sparrows from Kansas City to New York, back to Kansas City, to San Francisco--and he spotted these sparrows in each place--to Honolulu, to Shanghai, to I-ch'ang.

Q: Did he tell you this in the wardroom?

Captain Kretz: Yes.

Q: Amazing.

Captain Kretz: Yes. Oh, yes, he told us this in the wardroom, and here it is right here in a Los Angeles paper, half a page, a write-up on the whole story.

Q: Just for the record, I'm looking at a half-page of Sunday supplement, probably about 1936. It's an illustrated story with photographs of Mrs. Holton. The story is about the Holtons feeding little birds on board the USS _Panay_, and evidently the birds became accustomed to this; it's an exceptional story. I'll let the captain carry on.

Captain Kretz: Well, every morning around 10:00 o'clock when we were in port where we could join our wives along the river, Mrs. Holton would come down to the ship in her pink dress and pink parasol. And at that time, the chief wardroom steward had to have two baskets of sugar cookies ready. The captain would take one on his arm, and Mrs. Holton would take one on her arm, and they would go all over the ship crumpling up crumbs for these sparrows. Of course, not only those sparrows, but every sparrow in China tried to get aboard ship. They messed up the ship, so the executive officer would get mad and try to clean up the ship, and then the captain would put the executive officer under hack.* And this went on for months.

Q: Didn't the crew think this was rather odd?

Captain Kretz: The crew laughed at it.

Q: Well, how did you have any morale on board with this eccentric as a skipper?

Captain Kretz: Well, he didn't bother the crew too much. He didn't bother the crew; it was just the officers.

---

*Under hack refers to suspending an officer from duty and confining him to his stateroom.

Kretz #1 - 20

Q: How was the atmosphere in the wardroom at meals?

Captain Kretz: Oh, it was awful.

Q: Tense?

Captain Kretz: Tense.

Q: Nobody talking? Thoroughly unsatisfactory.

Captain Kretz: Very unsatisfactory.

Q: What happened eventually to this skipper?

Captain Kretz: Well, eventually, Steinbauer was transferred. Steinbauer, as the executive officer, could not get along with the skipper, as I have previously stated. Then he was ordered transferred from the ship. At the time, the ship was anchored in the Yangtze River, and the captain gave strict orders that there would be no celebrating his detachment. Particularly in China at that time, for any event, the Chinese would always have numerous fireworks, firecrackers to go off. So I happened to have the duty at the time Steinbauer was detached, and the captain told me to be sure there were no fireworks. I said, "There can't be any fireworks. We're anchored out here in the river, and I don't see how there can be any fireworks." But as soon as Steinbauer left the ship and got in the boat, numerous sampans appeared from just about everywhere, and all of them were loaded with fireworks, because the crew really liked the executive officer.

Q: So the Chinese had a Fourth of July celebration?

Captain Kretz: Which they do for any big celebration. So the captain immediately got ahold of me and threatened me with all sorts of dire things. I told him then that I'd had all I could take, and I wasn't going to take any more. If necessary, I was going to resign, but before I resigned, I was going to write a letter to the Commander in Chief of the Asiatic Fleet and tell him everything that I knew that was going on in that ship since the day I reported, which I did.

Q: How long was your letter?

Captain Kretz: A couple of pages. And I did this under the window of Lieutenant Ford, who was studying for his promotion examination as a lieutenant at the time, so that I'd have a witness when I told the captain that I was writing this letter.*
The captain tried every way he possibly could to prevent me from

---
*Lieutenant (junior grade) Robert S. Ford, USN, who had replaced Mothersill as the engineer officer.

Kretz #1 - 22

writing or mailing that letter, but I did take it ashore and mailed it. As soon as it reached Shanghai, we received orders to proceed immediately to Shanghai, and he was relieved.

Q: He was called aboard the flagship?

Captain Kretz: Called aboard the flagship and relieved of command.

Q: Who took command?

Captain Kretz: Lieutenant Bourke came aboard.*

Q: That took a lot of moral courage for you to do that, since nobody else had bothered to do it.

Captain Kretz: Nobody else would do it.

Q: Did you go aboard the flagship and talk to the staff later?

Captain Kretz: No, and they never called me.

Q: And I gather that you were the first to put down in writing the things that people had been talking about but nobody had the

---

*Lieutenant Richard J. Bourke, Jr., USN, had become executive officer and navigator following the departure of Steinbauer.

courage to put down in words.

Captain Kretz: That is true. That is absolutely true.

Q: What happened to Lieutenant Commander Holton?

Captain Kretz: At that time he was transferred down to Cavite for observation at the hospital in Cavite. From there, he was transferred back for a short period of time aboard the Black Hawk, which was a destroyer tender. And later he was transferred back to the United States, where the last I heard, he and his wife were both in St. Elizabeth's.*

Q: They were sort of mentally incapacitated, you'd say. Well, I suppose that the real villain in this would be a detail officer who ordered a person, who must have had eccentric characteristics before, to command of a gunboat in the Yangtze.

Captain Kretz: This information appeared in the papers all over the United States, right here in the paper. I think this was the Los Angeles Examiner.

Q: Captain, at the time of your cruise on the Yangtze, the

---

*St. Elizabeth's is a mental hospital in Washington, D.C.

Chinese Communists were beginning to make their presence felt. Chiang Kai-shek was the ruler of China. Can you tell us something about the relationship you had with Chiang Kai-shek's forces and how it went?

Captain Kretz: Chiang Kai-shek, at that time, had been kidnapped by the Communists and was held some place in North China--I don't remember where. He was finally released, and when he was released, the *Panay* was the station ship in Nanking, which at that time was the capital of China. At that time, one of my assigned duties was intelligence officer. I had to make a weekly intelligence report to Commander in Chief of the Asiatic Fleet. So I covered the release of General Chiang Kai-shek into Nanking, and I went ashore, and I mingled around with the people, and I was astounded to see how they sincerely welcomed his release and welcomed him back to Nanking. At that time, we didn't know whether the Chinese really wanted him or not, but after that, there was no question in my mind. And I put in my report that the Chinese were very sincerely grateful to have him back in Nanking.

Q: Did you get any help on your intelligence reports from our consul or embassy at Nanking?

Captain Kretz: Very little.

Q: You tried, obviously.

Captain Kretz: I'll tell you something about our embassy. One of my other jobs was to prepare evacuation plans for American citizens from all of the towns along the Yangtze River, which I did. When I got down to Nanking, we had to go completely from scratch, because we had had a legation there and now we had an embassy, and it was a new location. We had to have new plans. So I went out to the embassy and discussed with them how these plans should be made and how would be the best way to get the embassy people out. I said, "It appears to me there's a stream going down [I think it was on the east side of Nanking] alongside the wall." I thought that maybe we could get in it and maybe get a boat up that little stream and it would be a nice place to evacuate these people. But I said, "We don't have any maps, anything showing anything about it."

They said, "Well, we don't either."

And so I said, "I'll go over there and look at it." I took a bicycle, and I went over there. I put the bicycle up at the end of this stream, a ditch. I went down to this ditch. I got down there, and I was in the middle of a Chinese Army installation and they start shooting at me. I ran back up this ditch and got back on my bicycle. I went back to the embassy.

You know what those people said? "You had no damn business going down there in the first place."

Kretz #1 - 26

Q: They knew that it was dangerous and they didn't tell you? They let you go?

Captain Kretz: I don't know whether they knew if it was dangerous or not, but they said I had no business going down there in the first place.

Q: So you gave up on the embassy staff.

Captain Kretz: That's right. I had given up on them before that.

Q: Did you ever participate in an evacuation drill?

Captain Kretz: No.

Q: So you missed that.

Captain Kretz: After I had reported to the embassy what I found with this Chinese installation, they said, "Well, all you have to do is go back to the ship and fire that big 3-inch gun you have once, and these Chinese will all run for the hills."

Q: Simple solution.

Captain Kretz: Simple solution.

Q: Crazy!

Captain Kretz: But that was their attitude.

Q: Captain, after your experience with being shot at by the Chinese Army and the failure of the embassy staff to warn you, did you have any other relationships with the embassy staff?

Captain Kretz: Yes, I had relations with the embassy staff because I handled their communications. They had no radio and we had the only radio. The station ship in Nanking was always the communication ship for the embassy. The communication officer acted as the communication officer with the embassy and worked with the embassy on communication matters. We had some problems with them, because they would send their coded messages down by Chinese messenger to the ship. We would transmit them, as I remember it, directly to Manila, and then they'd be relayed back to the United States. In other words, before they reached Washington, they probably had been relayed two or three times.

The embassy was getting complaints from their people in Washington, the State Department, because of the poor quality of their messages and the difficulty of decoding them for so many mistakes.

Kretz #1 - 28

Q: Too many garbles.

Captain Kretz: Too many garbles. So the embassy blamed it on me.

Q: Impossible!

Captain Kretz: So I said, "All right." I sent back to the communication center in Washington and asked them if they would send me back the copies as they received them. And they sent back the whole works, and I'd check them. We'd made very few mistakes. Oh, the embassy got mad at me. God, they got mad! Because we wrote them a letter from the ship and sent it. They had written a letter about me and sent a copy to Commander in Chief of the Asiatic Fleet. So we wrote a letter and sent a copy to Commander in Chief of the Asiatic Fleet, with the copies of the messages.

And one Sunday morning--I remember this so clearly--a Chinese messenger came down from the embassy, and he had a regular big manila envelope. I met him at the gangway and he handed me this envelope. It wasn't sealed. I opened the envelope and it was a secret message. The plain language was there, the coding work sheets were there, and the encoded copy was there.

Q: Complete compromise.

Kretz #1 - 29

Captain Kretz: Complete compromise.

Q: Isn't that awful.

Captain Kretz: I reported it immediately, and I immediately sent a dispatch to Commander in Chief Asiatic Fleet, explaining what had happened. Because I knew they were going to try to blame it on me. Oh, boy, that thing really hit the fan.

Q: I hope somebody was censured.

Captain Kretz: I hope they were, too. We left before there was any more about it.

Q: Captain, to illustrate your point that the embassy staff was not as efficient as it should be in communication matters, I'm looking at a letter that you kept in your files from the Embassy of the United States of America at Nanking, dated 25 January 1937. It says:

"Dear Lieutenant Kretz:

I have received your communication of January 22, 1937, in regard to two telegrams which were delivered by the embassy messenger to the USS Oahu on January 21 instead of to the USS Panay. I have reminded the three embassy messengers that all telegrams are to be delivered to the USS Panay until they are instructed to the contrary. Thank you for bringing this matter to my attention.

Very truly yours,

Clayson W. Aldridge."

Captain, as you know, the American missionaries went into China in the latter part of the 19th Century in greater numbers and set up their own missions, the Catholics and the various Protestant denominations. What were your relationships with the missionaries?

Captain Kretz: As I said before, we did meet two Catholic nuns who had been captured by the Chinese and later released. I guess somebody paid their ransom. And I think there was a Catholic priest there that night, but the captain of the Wulin had them aboard.

Q: Were they Americans?

Captain Kretz: I was quite impressed with those people, but in my duty of preparing evacuation plans for them, I didn't think that they were very cooperative.

Q: Now you're speaking of missionaries as a class? Never mind the denomination?

Kretz #1 - 31

Captain Kretz: That's right, never mind the denomination.

Q: Specifically, did you go up to the missions and try to talk to them?

Captain Kretz: Oh, yes. Yes.

Q: What happened?

Captain Kretz: Well, I would tell them what we were trying to do, and that in case of an emergency, what we would try to do to rescue them and what they were supposed to do. And they didn't seem to be too interested.

Q: Sort of living in a world of their own--the Lord will provide.

Captain Kretz: Of course, they were living behind their walls and were isolated from the local people.

Q: I don't think they had an understanding of the political situation, do you?

Captain Kretz: I don't think they did either. I don't think they had the least understanding of what was really going on.

Kretz #1 - 32

Q: The missionaries that you met, were they long-timers in China?

Captain Kretz: Some were, and some were not. But some had been there quite some time.

Q: It was the custom of the foreign navies--U.S. Navy and British Navy, at least--to leave Shanghai and Manila and go up to Chefoo, North China, for the summer months where it was much cooler. Did you see any missionaries on vacation up there?

Captain Kretz: Yes, a lot of missionaries would come up there during the summer for vacation in Chefoo. Now, whether they went to other cities like Wei-hai-wei or Tsingtao, I don't know, but they did come to Chefoo.

Q: And I gather they left their flock to survive during the summer without them?

Captain Kretz: I don't know how they could have done anything else.

Q: So in the long run, the Christian missionary effort in China, you think, is questionable in terms of results. Is that a fair assessment?

Captain Kretz: Well, it is in a way. I do think that they helped in one way, of rescuing a lot of Chinese girl babies that would be left on their doorsteps or pushed through a door or something like that, and I think they did a lot in that respect.

Q: That's certainly worthwhile. Do you have any other comments to make on your experiences with missionaries, Captain?

Captain Kretz: Well, they called upon us, and they were very pleasant people. They must have been just as homesick at times as we were. I have very few comments to make about the missionaries other than the ones I've already given.

Q: Captain, I-ch'ang had how many people, would you say?

Captain Kretz: I would say approximately 15,000. It's a pure guess.

Q: And you had a polyglot population of white Russians and Eurasians and Chinese?

Captain Kretz: Yes, some. Not to too great an extent at I-ch'ang.

Q: Did you have white Russians there?

Kretz #1 - 34

Captain Kretz: Some, but nothing like, say, Hankow.

Q: What I'm getting at, I think, is that the enlisted men on board ship didn't have very much to do. They could go ashore on liberty and go to a bar and drink beer and maybe meet a white Russian girl and that was about it.

Captain Kretz: Or a Chinese girl, and that was it, yes.

Q: And how was your VD rate?* Not excessive?

Captain Kretz: Not excessive.

Q: Did they play baseball or any of those sports?

Captain Kretz: Yes, they had their sports and up in the compound they had some places where they could play games, ball.

Q: Do you have a feel for how long would an enlisted man stay on the China station? Did they have a limit--eight years?

Captain Kretz: Some stayed almost forever. They never wanted to come back.

―――――――――――――
*VD--venereal disease.

Kretz #1 - 35

Q: I guess there was no limit. Some of them retired out there.

Captain Kretz: Yes, some of them did retire out there, yes.

Q: Thank you, Captain. I think we'll pick up on the interviews next week.

Interview Number 2 with Captain Charles Henry Kretz, Jr.,
U.S. Navy (Retired)

Place: Captain Kretz's home in San Mateo, California

Date: 3 April 1984

Subject: U.S. Asiatic Fleet

Interviewer: Captain Paul B. Ryan, U.S. Navy (Retired)

Q: We are about to discuss Captain Kretz's cruise on the Yangtze Patrol in China in the latter part of the 1930s. At this time, conditions were very tense politically, and the then-Lieutenant (junior grade) Kretz had a bird's-eye, firsthand view of things. Captain, the last time, we were discussing how you spent your off-duty hours. You mentioned something about pheasant and duck hunting. Do you want to elaborate on that?

Captain Kretz: Yes, I would like to elaborate on that a little. Let's take the duck hunting first. As you know, the Yangtze River was just covered with wild ducks and geese because the Chinese had--for hunting them, they would trap them, and in some cases on a small lake they'd set up big things and kill a whole lot of them at one time, which they'd take to market and sell. So we used to take the boat over, the little ship's boat, on the banks of the river and go duck hunting. We did very well on the duck hunting, but when you'd get it back to the ship, the doctor would be waiting for us. Before we even got off the boat, really, he'd herd us all up to sick bay, where we got a complete alcohol bath. The reason for this is that a few years before or a year or so before, some British officers had gone duck hunting and they came down with schistosomiasis and died. Schistosomiasis was a disease caused by small worms that lived in the mud around the Yangtze River. They would bore under the skin, and once they got into the bloodstream, at that time there was no cure. There was no possible way of removing them once they got into the bloodstream.

Q: Did you have specific cases of people dying from this?

Captain Kretz: Yes, British naval officers died from schistosomiasis.

Q: So when you shot ducks, what was your bag, generally? Did you come back with ten?

Captain Kretz: About ten or so. We didn't overdo it.

Q: So you had enough for the wardroom dinners.

Captain Kretz: Enough for the wardroom dinner, yes.

Q: What about pheasants?

Captain Kretz: When we arrived at Wuhu on one trip, the manager came down to the dock and told us that there was a Chinese cemetery at the compound and that it was just loaded with pheasants. He wanted to know whether any of us wanted to go pheasant hunting. So the ship's doctor, Leslie Ekvall, and myself decided we would go pheasant hunting.* We got back into the cemetery and found it was really loaded with pheasants. They were just everywhere, but there were coffins on top of the ground. As you know, the Chinese rarely buried their dead. They just put the coffins out and put them on top of the ground, and unless they were very lucky, they let them lay. If they were wealthy, they'd have some dirt thrown on the coffin.

So at one time, several pheasants got up in front of us, and Dr. Ekvall jumped on top of one of these coffins to get a better shot. And it caved in, and he went right through the coffin into something that was very ripe. But we did kill enough pheasants that day to feed the crew.

Q: How many in the crew?

Captain Kretz: There were 54, as I remember.

Q: With five officers, that's quite a lot of pheasants.

---
*Lieutenant (junior grade) Leslie D. Ekvall, Medical Corps, USN.

Kretz #2 - 39

Captain Kretz: It was a lot of pheasants, yes.

Q: Why didn't the Chinese eat pheasants?

Captain Kretz: They did. They would trap them, but they didn't have any guns to shoot them. They would trap them, as they did ducks and other things that they used to trap. I guess they trapped them. Another thing was snipe. They would serve the snipe with the head on so you could tell it was snipe and wasn't something else.

Q: This was a roast, baked snipe?

Captain Kretz: Yes, roast. Roast snipe. I used to have them quite often as hors d'oeuvres before dinner.

Q: You mentioned also in our previous discussion a trip to the cemetery at early morning. What was that?

Captain Kretz: That trip was done on Easter morning of 1936. We had just arrived in China and were on our way up the Yangtze River in the British riverboat Wulin, and she stopped for a couple of hours in Wuhu. My wife and I decided to go ashore and walk around and try to get an idea of what inland China was really like. Of course, in those days, when you went ashore in

China, you always carried canes--mainly to protect yourself from dogs. We looked around and went through the town and went outside the town out by the cemetery, and there were many dogs in the cemetery, rooting in the cemetery where there were skeletons around, and the dogs were chewing on the bones. It was a very unpleasant Easter morning for us.

Q: I suppose life is relatively cheap in China, and this was another manifestation of that.

Captain Kretz: I can give you another one while we're on this. One time--I think this was in Hankow, we saw an overturned junk, a large junk, floating down the river, and I think there were three or four Chinese sitting on the bottom. It was followed by many, many sampans and the ones in the sampans would make no attempt to rescue the people sitting on the top of the boat. They were waiting until they fell off and they died so they could seize the boat. That's an idea of the cheapness of life in China.

Q: I guess there's no such thing as charity or mercy?

Captain Kretz: No, they felt that if they rescued someone and saved their life, they'd have to take care of them the rest of their lives.

Kretz #2 - 41

Q: Yes, that is a Chinese custom, I know.

Captain Kretz: I saw another instance of that in Nanking when I was standing on the deck of the Panay, waiting to go ashore. Our boat was in the beach. And waiting for it to return, I was looking right at the pontoon on the shore. A junk unloading five-gallon cans of gasoline exploded, and I can still see these bodies flying through the air. The whole river caught on fire. There was another American gunboat--I think it was the Oahu, I'm not sure--tied up to a pontoon downriver from this explosion. And the gasoline was floating down towards this ship and also Chinese in the water. We tried to rescue the Chinese. We did rescue some with our boat and took them ashore, but the Chinese would have nothing to do with them. They wouldn't come near them after we took them ashore.

Q: Because they'd be responsible for them for life?

Captain Kretz: Yes.

Q: Captain, I understand you have two children. One was born in China during your cruise there. How did you find out that you were a father?

Captain Kretz: I was in Hankow at the time. It was on the 15th of April 1937. I had to go ashore on some official business; what it was now I do not remember. I went ashore and got a rickshaw and went up into town and accomplished my business. When I returned a short time later, all of the rickshaw coolies came running out to me and said, "Master, Missy has catched a very fine young master." And I didn't know how they knew this, but I got to the ship and they had just received a dispatch that my son had been born. It shows you how fast information traveled on the Yangtze River.

Q: So the coolies were the bearers of glad tidings.

Captain Kretz: Yes. They found things out so fast.

Q: Where was the baby born?

Captain Kretz: In Shanghai.

Q: In a hospital?

Captain Kretz: Country hospital.

Q: Did your family stay on with you now that the baby was born?

Captain Kretz: Yes, yes, they did.

Kretz #2 - 43

Q: But he immediately acquired an amah, I suppose.

Captain Kretz: Yes.

Q: Did the Navy doctors check him occasionally?

Captain Kretz: Oh, yes, yes.

Q: So you were very happy with the medical care?

Captain Kretz: Oh, yes, I was very happy with the medical care.

Q: This hospital, did it have a civilian staff?

Captain Kretz: Yes, it did.

Q: Americans?

Captain Kretz: It was a civilian hospital, and I think it was multinational personnel.

Q: Was it there to serve the foreign community--the French, the British, the Italians and so forth?

Captain Kretz: As far as I know, yes.

Q: I see. Where did you find living quarters with your new addition?

Captain Kretz: We had a room in the Cathay Mansions.

Q: And that was sufficient?

Captain Kretz: Oh, yes.

Q: Captain, the China of the 1930s was rife with banditry and lawlessness and fighting, so security was a problem. What measures did you take to safeguard your family in these quarters ashore?

Captain Kretz: The only place that we had any real problem was in Hankow, and it wasn't too bad for us. I remember in the Central Hotel a coolie would put his bunk across the entrance doorway every night so that the only way you could get into the hotel was to crawl over his bunk, which would wake him up. That was the only security that we had.

Q: Did everybody use this method of guard?

Captain Kretz: The only place I know of was the Central Hotel.

Q: That must have been not a very secure place, then.

Captain Kretz: Well, we didn't have much problem with the Chinese.

Q: What about thievery? Was that pretty common?

Captain Kretz: Yes, thievery was common. You had to take care of what you had and watch it very closely, but it wasn't too bad.

Q: This brings up a point about on board ship. You had a lot of Chinese on board ship. Did you ever experience any cases of theft or pilferage?

Captain Kretz: Yes, I did. I was working in my room one night and I had the watch. I guess I was the only officer on board, and I had some money that I'd taken out of my pocket and I'd put on my desk. I went out of the room--I was called out for something. I wasn't gone more than two or three minutes, and I went back and all my money was gone. But I think that was taken by a crew member. In fact, I had pretty good suspicions, but not enough to make a charge.

Q: Captain, one of the traditions of the Navy of the 1930s was that wherever one was, one listened by radio to the Army-Navy

Kretz #2 - 46

game, and it was usually played in Philadelphia. At the Academy as a midshipman, I remember hearing stories of the China station having the Army officers and the naval officers in the same club watching a giant replica of a playing field and moving the ball back and forth to follow the course of the game by radio. Do you have any recollections of this?

Captain Kretz: I don't have any recollections of being in the club, but for the Army-Navy game in 1936, I rigged a radio on the roof of the Cathay Mansions. I was able to pick up Manila. So on the night of the Army-Navy game, Bob Ford--now Rear Admiral Ford--and I went up on the roof about 2:00 o'clock in the morning, and we tuned in the Army-Navy game. We sat up there the rest of the night listening to the Army-Navy game, and all the Chinese in the hotel thought we were crazy. But we did get to hear the Army-Navy game.

Q: Just the two of you up there all night.

Captain Kretz: Bob's wife, Edie, came up.

Q: Did you fortify yourself with spirits?

Captain Kretz: Oh, yes, we fortified ourselves quite well during that time.

Q: By the way, I presume you know Admiral Bob Ford lives in San Mateo, doesn't he?

Captain Kretz: I know him very well.

Q: He's a neighbor of yours, practically.

Captain Kretz: Yes, he's right up here. We've been close for years, ever since we were in China.

Q: I hope he knows about Admiral Kemp Tolley's association with the Yang Pat Patrollers.*

Captain Kretz: If he doesn't, I'm going to let him know.

Q: Good. I know Admiral Tolley would be glad to hear that.

Captain, by 1937, the political situation was becoming very taut, and in August the Japanese bombed Shanghai and sent troops ashore, and there was heavy fighting and loss of life there. The Japanese had already taken Manchuria, starting in 1932, and then they had the troops come down from North China into Peking after

---

*Rear Admiral Kemp Tolley, USN(Ret.), is the subject of a Naval Institute oral history which covers his experiences on the China station. Tolley is also the author of Yangtze Patrol: The U.S. Navy in China (Annapolis, Maryland: Naval Institute Press, 1971).

the Marco Polo Bridge incident.* So did you sense that things were becoming particularly dangerous, and did you see any bloodshed?

Captain Kretz: We sensed that it was very dangerous for a long time. The <u>Bulmer</u> was the first ship ordered down to Shanghai after the Japanese marines landed, which was on the 11th of July 1937.

Q: Were you aboard the <u>Bulmer</u> then?

Captain Kretz: I was aboard the <u>Bulmer</u> then, yes.

Q: You were transferred, then, from the <u>Panay</u> in 1937.

Captain Kretz: In '37.

Q: And you were ordered to the <u>Bulmer</u> to be gunnery officer?

Captain Kretz: Well, I was first lieutenant and had several jobs during that period of time.

---

*On 7 July 1937, on the pretext of Chinese interference with a minor Japanese military maneuver near the Marco Polo Bridge in the Peking area, the Japanese began their attack on China. Peking fell on 29 July. The Sino-Japanese War later broadened with the onset of World War II and did not really end until 1945.

Q: So just before we leave the Panay, were you glad to go aboard a bigger ship and more responsibility?

Captain Kretz: Well, yes, I wanted to get into destroyers and I had requested destroyers.

Q: So this was really a good break.

Captain Kretz: The normal tour of duty at that time on the Yangtze River was one year.

Q: One year. I see. That's about routine, and then you went to a bigger ship.

Captain Kretz: Then you went to a larger ship.

Q: So you reported aboard the Bulmer, and you were about to mention an incident of bloodshed, I believe.

Captain Kretz: Yes. We proceeded immediately from Chefoo to Shanghai and arrived during the actual landing of the Japanese at Woosung. We went right through the Japanese fleet as they were bombarding the shore, with troops along the shore and landing craft on the beach and on the shore. We were right in the middle of the combat, with shells flying around all around us.

Kretz #2 - 50

We proceeded on up the Whangpoo River to the Texaco compound, where we moored to a pontoon and were to guard the Texaco compound. We were there for months.

Q: You were maintaining a presence there.

Captain Kretz: Maintaining a presence and we were right in the midst of most of the fighting. It was all around us.

Q: Is this the incident of where you saw a loss of life?

Captain Kretz: We saw loss of life all the time.

Q: You were watching from the ship with your binoculars, and you could see bombing taking place.

Captain Kretz: From the ship. The whole thing, yes. They were landing right near us, with antiaircraft landing all over us, landing on the ship and around us. Fortunately, we only had one man that was wounded, and that was a very slight wound from a machine gun bullet, flesh wound.

Q: Stray bullet?

Captain Kretz: Yes, stray bullet. Other than that, we were

lucky. We were right in the middle of this thing. The Japanese would come up with their destroyers and cruisers firing point-blank into the opposite bank of the river. When they'd get near us, they'd stop firing, turn around and salute us, and as soon as they passed, open fire again.

Q: So they rendered passing honors and then opened fire again.

Captain Kretz: Opened fire, yes.

Q: Really astounding.

Captain Kretz: I remember one day I was in the boat going up to Shanghai, and just a little ways up the river from the Texaco compound, the river was literally covered with bodies of men, women, and children.

Q: Bombing?

Captain Kretz: No, they were massacred.

Q: Machine gun bullets?

Captain Kretz: No, I'll explain it. They all had their hands tied behind their backs. Some of them had been shot in the head, some of them had their limbs cut off. Some of them apparently had just been pushed in and drowned. I took a whole roll of film, which I later developed myself. I kept that roll of film for quite some time. This may be a little bit of interest to you. The <u>Bulmer</u> was ordered to make a trip to Yokohama to meet one of the Dollar liners that was bringing our mail from the United States.* At that time the Japanese were transporting our mail and were censoring our mail before we got it from Shanghai.

Q: They were opening the mail.

Captain Kretz: Opening the mail, yes. So we were sent over for the first trip. We made many others after that. We picked up this mail directly from the Dollar liner to bring it back to Shanghai. When we got to Yokohama, I went up to the embassy in Tokyo. I took these pictures up with me, and I showed these pictures to the people in the embassy, and their comments were, "Oh, the Japanese would never do anything like that. The Chinese have done it to try to get sympathy." And that is the truth.

Q: Did you retain the film?

Captain Kretz: I retained those pictures for a number of years,

---
*The Dollar Line operated commercial passenger ships in the area. Its smokestack marking was a dollar sign.

and I remember one night my wife and I were sitting before a fireplace and we looked at them. It was so revolting, we said we'd never look at those pictures again, and we threw them in the fireplace. I guess I should have retained them, but they were awful.

Q: Historically I guess you're right, you should have. But tell me, at the embassy, we had a naval attache. Did it occur to you to look him up?

Captain Kretz: No, I don't remember who I talked to in the embassy. I talked to several people, but I was only there for a short period, because I had to get up to Tokyo and then get back to the ship. But that was the reaction I got from the people at the embassy.

Q: Surprising, I must say. In 1937, President Roosevelt ordered about 1,800 Marines to Shanghai. Did you see any Marines in Shanghai of this contingent?

Captain Kretz: Yes, we already had the 4th Marines in Shanghai, and this other contingent of Marines came out on the light cruiser Marblehead; they came up to Shanghai.

Q: Did they have a stabilizing presence?

Captain Kretz: I don't know whether they had a stabilizing presence or not. They had a lot of observation posts. I went up to one one day. It was on top of a building at Soochow Creek.* At that time the Japanese were fighting in the streets down below and were trying to take the railway station. They were bombing the railroad station. We were up there watching this action. I was with the 4th Marines, and they were going to take me up and show me this thing. Bombers were coming over and we could tell when they were going to drop their bombs. One plane came over and it didn't let go, and it didn't let go, and finally I thought, "Oh, my God, we're going to get that one." Actually, the bomb went over us and landed in the street in front of this building, right in the middle of a crowded street of Chinese.

Q: The Marines were there to guard U.S. citizens and U.S. property, which I suppose was mostly in the foreign sector. So they didn't move outside the perimeter where the fighting was really taking place?

Captain Kretz: No, I don't think they ever did.

Q: There was a group of civilians known as the "Shanghai Guards," I believe. They were U.S.-British businessmen, among

---
*There is a useful map of Shanghai on page 241 of Tolley's _Yangtze Patrol_.

Kretz #2 - 55

others, who were trained to shoot a gun and fight if necessary. Did you ever see any of these people?

Captain Kretz: No, I did not. After the war started, the only time I got to Shanghai would be for very short periods.* My wife was there for quite a while.

Q: I know that you weren't ashore too much, so you might not have seen this, but there are occasions reported where Japanese soldiers slapped and stripped U.S. citizens ashore in China. But you didn't witness any of these episodes.

Captain Kretz: No, I didn't see any of that.

Q: But events fell apart so much that the U.S. Government finally decided to evacuate U.S. wives and children from China.

Captain Kretz: Yes.

Q: Would you elaborate on that?

Captain Kretz: Yes. At the time, my wife and son were still in Chefoo. They were evacuated--I think it was on the Canopus--and

---

*This is a reference, of course, to the Sino-Japanese war.

brought down to Shanghai, stopped in Shanghai for an overnight period, tied up at the Texaco compound.* We had gone out in the Bulmer and escorted the ship in. Then they proceeded on down to Manila.

Q: Back home aboard a Dollar liner?

Captain Kretz: No, my wife stayed in Manila until the next spring. Then she returned to Shanghai and lived in the Clement Apartments in the French sector.

Q: Mrs. Kretz, while you're here, perhaps you can describe your stay in Manila when the ship was in China.

Mrs. Kretz: May I read part of it?

Q: Fine, just go ahead and read it.

Mrs. Kretz: The next letter is dated November 15, 1937 from Baguio, Philippines. "There are some things of interest I'd like to record. On the 14th of August 1937, the Sino-Japanese War began, and our comfortable life was changed. Scotty, your godfather, hurried from his ship to get back there with the

---

*The USS Canopus (AS-9) was a submarine tender attached to the U.S. Asiatic Fleet.

announcement, 'Kiss your wife goodbye, the ship is leaving.'* I didn't see dad for months. Our bags were packed for weeks, ready for evacuation. The Navy tried to persuade me to take the baby home, but since our tour was for over a year more, I was able to stay. We were evacuated from Chefoo to Manila aboard a Navy transport. There were two bunks in my room, one with a bassinette roped to it. All the young wives washed diapers and so forth by hand and hung them in a bathroom. Getting to the johns was an ordeal of wet diapers and so forth hanging from all sorts of lines.

"The ship stopped in Shanghai where dad proved to be a hero by going through shell fire to bring some disposable diapers aboard. Thank God those had been invented! There was a battle that night between the Japanese and Chinese, and this time the firecrackers were real."

Q: Mrs. Kretz, you're mentioning your escape from Shanghai. On your arrival in Manila with the other group of young naval wives and mothers, how did you ladies carry on?

Mrs. Kretz: We carried on like Navy wives--we did the best we could with what we had. And Lieutenant Steinbauer had sent one

---

*"Scotty" is a reference to Lieutenant (junior grade) Reader C. Scott, USN, who was assigned to Kretz's ship, the USS <u>Bulmer</u> (DD-222).

message after another up to Baguio in the Philippines, trying to find me a place to stay. Manila was so overcrowded, there was absolutely no place.

Q: Baguio was a summer resort in the mountains.

Mrs. Kretz: Yes. Absolutely gorgeous. So Edie met me with my baby in Manila.

Q: That's Mrs. Ford.

Mrs. Kretz: That's Mrs. Ford. And put me on the train later that day and we went up to Baguio where they had cottages for us.

Q: The Navy rented the cottages, so to speak, or leased them? Or did you individually lease them?

Captain Kretz: We paid for them.

Mrs. Kretz: We paid for them.

Q: I see. But the Navy reserved them, so to speak?

Mrs. Kretz: I believe so, yes.

Kretz #2 - 59

Q: You were there for several months?

Mrs. Kretz: We were there for several months, and at first I think there were about five of us in one cottage. It was rather isolated, and we came home from dinner one night and one of the wives screamed, "Anne, there's a man coming in my window!" He got out when the four of us came in, and we called, and they sent a guard up who stayed there all night. The next day they transferred us to smaller cottages in a group where we were much more comfortable.

Q: And safer.

Mrs. Kretz: Much safer.

Q: Baguio has a nice golf course. Did you play golf?

Mrs. Kretz: Well, I tried to. It was a beautiful course, and I have some descriptions in here.

Q: Mrs. Kretz, do you have any particular recollections of Baguio other than the security aspect?

Mrs. Kretz: Yes, I have. It was one of the most beautiful places we have ever lived. This is a letter dated November 15,

1937, Camp John Hay, Baguio, Philippine Islands. "It's gorgeous up here. There are miles of mountains, trails, verdant things, flowers, plants and so forth. We have a golf course, tennis, walking, valleys to explore, and the fascinating natives. The Benguets, or is it the Bontoc tribe, wear G-strings and long coats. Mestizas, I think, are half-white and half-native and stunningly beautiful. The Lavanderas carry our clothes on their heads and walk beautifully, and just lately, the dining room boys have worn pants. In the rice fields two days from here, the fields are tilled as they were 4,000 years ago, and the natives bite money to see if it's edible. They only want matches; flint is too hard to make fire. I wish I could take that trip to Bontoc and Banque." I later did.

Q: Captain, in October of 1937, President Roosevelt made a famous speech known as the quarantine speech in Chicago.* The theme of his talk was that the United States will not tolerate international gangsterism and that the free world must "take positive endeavors to preserve peace." In this sense, he was hinting that Japan would suffer certain penalties, such as the embargo U.S. slapped on in varying degrees and gradually. Did you see any more aggressive and barbarous practices by the Japanese Army and Navy while you were aboard the Bulmer?

---
*For more on the quarantine speech, see "FDR's 'Big Stick,'" U.S. Naval Institute Proceedings, July 1980, pages 68-73.

Captain Kretz: Oh, yes, they were terrible. I've seen many headless bodies that would be left on the top of a pontoon for days and weeks.

Q: You were moored to a buoy?

Captain Kretz: We were moored to a pontoon at the Texaco compound.

Q: I see. So you were really tied up to the beach, then.

Captain Kretz: Yes, we were tied up to the beach, but we'd have to go into Shanghai periodically to do something or other. I can remember right on the Bund in Shanghai, the bodies of people the Japanese caught and would behead them and just leave them there. They were just ruthless.

Q: I gather that in this note here, you had something that was of interest.

Captain Kretz: There were so many bodies floating down the Whangpoo River that they would be caught between the bow of the ship and the pontoon, and the...

Q: Wedged in there.

Captain Kretz: Wedged in there, and a couple of times we had another destroyer tied up alongside of us. For quite a while we had a British destroyer tied up alongside of us, and we used the extra-duty men with bamboo poles to push these bodies out so we could go ahead and float down the river.

Q: That's really gruesome but necessary.

Captain Kretz: Necessary. There wasn't anything else you could do about it.

Q: Speaking of a British destroyer, in conversation with the Royal Navy, did you sense that eventually there would be war with Japan?

Captain Kretz: We all knew it.

Q: I see.

Captain Kretz: We very definitely knew it. When we came back from China in '38, I was telling everybody, "We're going to be at war with Japan in just a few years." And nobody would believe me.

Q: I understand that Admiral Harry Yarnell, who was CinC Asiatic

Fleet, requested the CNO, Admiral Leahy at the time, for more ships, but that President Roosevelt decided not to because of the strong isolationist sentiment in Congress and in the public.* Did you sense that the U.S. public was rather indifferent about what was going on in China at that time?

Captain Kretz: Yes, I think the only thing that aroused the public on what was going on in China at that time was the sinking of the Panay. I saw nothing else that seemed to arouse the public of the United States or the press.

Q: The Panay was sunk on 12 December 1937, on the upper reaches of the Yangtze.

Captain Kretz: Just up above Nanking, near Wuhu.

Q: Right. And what was your personal reaction to those shipmates on board?

Captain Kretz: I felt very sorry for them. At that time, on the 12th of December, the Bulmer was anchored in Tsingtao Harbor between two Japanese cruisers. When we heard of the sinking of

---

*Admiral Harry E. Yarnell, USN, Commander in Chief U.S. Asiatic Fleet from 30 October 1936 to 25 July 1939. Admiral William D. Leahy, USN, was Chief of Naval Operations from 2 January 1937 to 1 August 1939.

the <u>Panay</u>, we immediately put warheads on our torpedoes. We kept six torpedoes trained on each of these Japanese cruisers day and night.

Q: Did they show any resentment at this?

Captain Kretz: Oh, yes, but what could they do?

Q: Did they have their torpedoes trained on you, or guns?

Captain Kretz: They didn't have the torpedoes, but they had their guns. I guess they were trained on us. But if we weren't going to get out, there were two Japanese cruisers that weren't going to get out either.

Q: Good.

Captain Kretz: So at that time, the Japanese were just outside the harbor and were preparing for a landing at Tsingtao. We had some people on shore, particularly the diplomatic people in the consulate. We wanted to have some kind of contact with the shore. There was an American building owned by an American in Tsingtao, and we acquired the top floor of this building in downtown Tsingtao. I was ordered ashore as senior patrol officer. I have a letter here showing that. We sent ashore also radio equipment and some guns and ammunition.

Q: You were communicating with the ship from the shore?

Captain Kretz: Yes, communicating with the ship from the shore. I stayed there, I guess, about three days, and finally I was relieved. Actually, my roommate from the Naval Academy showed up, and I never knew where he came from.

Q: What was his name?

Captain Kretz: Bob Roblin.*

Q: What ship was he in, another destroyer?

Captain Kretz: He was in one of the gunboats, but I've forgotten which one.

Q: I see. Fine. I didn't mean to interrupt you there.

Captain Kretz: He just came up to me and said, "I've been ordered up here to relieve you and you're to get back on the ship immediately. They're waiting to get under way until you get back

---
*Lieutenant (junior grade) Robert D. Roblin, Jr., USN, who was assigned to the USS Sacramento (PG-19), an Asiatic Fleet gunboat.

aboard."

I got back aboard, and we headed directly down to Amoy, where the Japanese were landing.

Q: There again, you were to serve as a scout and report the activities.

Captain Kretz: Right.

Q: Did you stay in Amoy long?

Captain Kretz: Yes, I guess we were there a couple of weeks. The Japanese were firing over us at the beach on the other side, because they said there were Chinese over there. We didn't think there were. But then periodically, they'd land a shell as close to us as they possibly could, and so the captain and the exec both went ashore to complain to the Japanese command about firing so close to us. That left me in command of the ship, and the Japanese let one go right on our bow. I went to general quarters and aimed our 5-inch guns on this gun emplacement, which I could see not more than 500 yards from us. And they stopped firing on us.

Q: They were playing "chicken" with you.

Kretz #2 - 67

Captain Kretz: Yes, they were playing "chicken."

Q: Who was the skipper of the Bulmer?

Captain Kretz: Walter Ansel.*

Q: Who was the exec?

Captain Kretz: The exec at that time was Jack Burke, and Jack was killed in the South Dakota in the Savo Island Battle.**

Q: Did you receive any letters from home that gave you a sense of U.S. public opinion with regard to the Panay?

Captain Kretz: I received some letters from my mother. She was very concerned about us being over there, but nothing from public reaction in the United States.

Q: Aside from the initial outrage and the fact that Japan paid-- I think it was $2.2 million in reparations and apologized, there was really no long-lasting sense of anger on the part of the U.S.

---

*Lieutenant Commander Walter C. Ansel, USN, whose oral history is in the Naval Institute collection.
**Lieutenant John E. Burke, USN. As a lieutenant commander on board the South Dakota (BB-57), Burke was killed during a night surface battle with the Japanese the night of 14-15 November 1942 near Guadalcanal.

public regarding the Panay.

Captain Kretz: Not that I could see.

Q: It takes a long time for the U.S. public to react, and it takes Pearl Harbor, I suppose.

Captain Kretz: Yes.

Q: Captain, in addition to being gunnery officer of the Bulmer, you were also the commissary officer. Did you have any adventures in dealing with Chinese merchants in buying food for the crew and the like?

Captain Kretz: Yes. In late '37 or early '38, the Bulmer was sent up to North China, and it was anticipated at that time that the Asiatic Fleet would "summer" in North China--in Chefoo and Tsingtao, as they always had in the past. I was assigned the job of preparing the contract for provisions for the fleet for the summer. And I was furnished with copies of the old contract and some meager instructions. I worked up a contract with the Chinese merchants, and they all came in and put in their bids for everything. We knew that they had already made up their minds which one was going to get which contract. So actually, the bid didn't mean very much, but we did come up with a contract, and they seemed very, very anxious for me to sign this contract, in fact, so anxious that I became suspicious and refused to sign it. I said I wanted to take it back to the ship overnight and look it over. So they said, okay. I took it back to the ship and I had each officer on the ship read the contract and see if there was something wrong with it. No one could find anything wrong, but I knew from the actions of these Chinese that there was something in there that was out of line.

That night, I went over it, and then I went to bed. I turned in my bunk; I couldn't sleep. Finally, about 2:00 o'clock, I woke up and said, "I've got it!" I looked at the contract, and sure enough, they had left out one word, and that word was "butcher." It turned out that I was buying a bunch of cattle on the hoof instead of beef.

Q: And certainly the U.S. Navy couldn't use that beef.

Captain Kretz: No.

Q: Captain, the fact that you were tied up alongside British ships on the China station meant that occasionally you would be entertained with the King's wine mess. If you made an official call, I know that the custom of the British Navy is that the King's Government pays for the liquor, so they always like to open up new bottles. Did you have any experience with the

British Navy in this sense?

Captain Kretz: Yes, I had two experiences. One, the <u>Bulmer</u> was anchored in Chefoo. The British submarine, the <u>Proteus</u> came in, and I was sent over to make the official call, which was supposed to last approximately 10 to 15 minutes. This was in about 8:30 in the morning, and I didn't leave that ship until late in the afternoon, at which time the commanding officer sent a message on His Majesty's Service to my wife in Chefoo, telling her where I was.

Q: Can you read the message?

Captain Kretz: Yes. "This is to certify that Lootenant (j.g.) Henry Kretz has been detained on board the H.M.S. <u>Proteus</u>, cementing the friendship of the United States Navy and His Britannic Majesty's Navy and that he took departure at 15:05, Zone Minus Eight. Signed, with love, Jones."

Q: What rank was he?

Captain Kretz: He was a lieutenant commander.

Q: Or left-tenant commander, as they say.

Captain Kretz: Left-tenant commander in command. Later that evening, we all wound up in the club together. The other experience was in Shanghai when the Bulmer was guarding the Texaco compound. A British destroyer was also guarding a British compound, which was only a few hundred yards from us. Since we had the best food, and they had the booze, we decided they would join our wardroom mess, and we'd join their wine mess. And that worked out very well, except we decided we were too far apart. So finally, we tied the two ships up alongside each other so we could just walk across and go aboard and make it a little easier.

Q: That's good thinking. Tell me, did the British sailors fraternize with the U.S. sailors at all?

Captain Kretz: To some extent, yes.

Q: I suspect that there was no "splicing the main brace" with the U.S. sailors, even though you were tied up?*

Captain Kretz: No, no, no, there wasn't.

Q: Captain, if you survived relations with the British Navy, how did you manage to survive trying to obtain Chinese food? I mean

---

*Splicing the main brace is a reference to drinking of alcoholic beverages.

vegetables and fruit, with all the violence going on and the shooting, the killings. Did you have any adventures there?

Captain Kretz: Yes. As I mentioned earlier, we had a contract for vegetables and fruit and also for meat, but I have a letter here that I received from the Hop Yik Company in Chefoo, China. This is addressed to the Chief Steward, USS <u>Bulmer</u>, Number 222. And it states, "Did you remember the mail we wrote you regarding to the native cauliflowers in accordance with the contract opened on board the U.S.S. Black Hawk? We regret very much to inform you in about of this matter again. It is scarce of rain over Shantung Province almost nearly two months. This is why makes the native cauliflowers and cabbage even so small or bad. It is impossible for us to deliver to you in any way. We have made an inquiry on Dairen, but the answer says, 'cauliflowers of first term were out of season and the next term are small.' Again we try our best from the other port whether we can get a little from Tokyo, Formosa and Tientsin or not. The turnips are out of season too and we couldn't get any from the market. Thank you very much if you change your order for some else."

Q: Captain, one of the hazards for a ship's company on isolated duty, as in China, means that you probably will have problems in maintenance and upkeep of the engineering plant, in particular, and maybe hull cleaning and so forth. What did you do with regard to this problem?

Captain Kretz: Well, while we were on the river, there was a small shipyard located up the Whangpoo River beyond Shanghai. We went into this yard for minor overhaul. It wasn't anything major, but we did have trouble with the Chinese coming aboard and stealing things. In fact, we caught two or three. In the Bulmer, in December, just before the Panay was sunk, we went up to Tsingtao along with the Edsall, another four-piper destroyer, and went into a commercial dry dock for bottom cleaning. While we were in the dry dock, the Chinese mined the dry dock and were going to blow it up because the Japanese were preparing for landings in Tsingtao.

So we had to maintain armed guards all the way around the dry dock 24 hours a day in order to prevent the Chinese from blowing the dry dock up. As soon as we were out and we were anchored in the harbor at Tsingtao, the Chinese came out to be paid, and we paid them. They had all the proper papers. And then about an hour or two later, some more Chinese came out to be paid. The first ones were the bandits, and the other ones were legitimate, and we'd already paid the bandits!

Q: What happened then?

Captain Kretz: We paid it. We had a receipt. I don't know

whatever happened later on about it. They got the money and disappeared.

Q: Maybe the second group were bandits, too.

Captain Kretz: Maybe they were, too.

Q: Where did you have your main overhauls done?

Captain Kretz: At Cavite in the Philippines.

Q: On this detached duty, did you people on board have a chance to carry out routine training? We all remember the mandatory exercises and drills that we had to go through each quarter and each year, full-power runs and so forth. Did you have a chance to carry these out?

Captain Kretz: A few, but not very many. We were carrying them out.

Q: So Admiral Yarnell took a tolerant view of these regulations?

Captain Kretz: Yes.

Q: He knew that you had a job to do.

Kretz #2 - 75

Captain Kretz: Right.

Q: Captain, if I may, I'd like to ask a question of Mrs. Kretz. You were in the Philippines for some time. Did you ever come back to China?

Mrs. Kretz: Yes, we did. We came back before we were due to come home.

Q: Is that because conditions were safer?

Mrs. Kretz: Yes, they were at the time, and his tour of duty was up after two and a half years out there.

Q: With the Japanese controlling the city of Shanghai, did you require Japanese permission, a visa, for example, on your passport to enter China?

Mrs. Kretz: I think the visa I mentioned in the letter was for Japan, because I was going back to Shanghai and taking a boat-- I've forgotten the name of it--to Japan where I would stay for three or four days until the <u>President Coolidge</u> came in and he came back from the Philippines.

Q: I see then in April you returned to China from Manila, and you went via Hong Kong by commercial ship.

Mrs. Kretz: Yes, that is correct.

Q: And then on to Shanghai. The captain's tour was coming to a close. A three-year tour was routine, wasn't it, Captain, at the China station?

Captain Kretz: Two and a half years.

Q: During your last few months in China, were conditions normal, or did you run into any more crises?

Captain Kretz: I was in the Bulmer, and the Bulmer at that time was stationed in Olongapo, operating out of Olongapo, but my wife had returned to China, to Shanghai, before the Bulmer had returned to the Philippines. So since my tour of duty was about to expire, we decided that she would stay in Shanghai and meet me in Japan on my way home from the China station at the completion of my tour of duty out there. So she did, and during that time, she contracted paratyphoid and was very, very ill. Then after recovering, she did meet me in Yokohama, when the Coolidge arrived, and we came home on the Coolidge.

Q Captain, you've refreshed your memory of how you got from

Kretz #2 - 77

Chefoo to Shanghai to see Mrs. Kretz, who was in desperate straits, I gather, from this paratyphoid B.

Captain Kretz: Yes. I obtained leave from the commanding officer, but there was no transportation and no way I could get down to Shanghai, but fortunately, the Augusta came into Chefoo. The Augusta was the flagship of the Asiatic Fleet at that time. I went aboard the Augusta and talked to the staff and obtained permission to go to Shanghai aboard the Augusta.

I found my wife in very serious condition when I arrived in Shanghai, and she was a little improved the next week, and I had to return to the ship in Chefoo. So I took a Chinese passenger boat from Shanghai to Chefoo. En route, we stopped to unload some cargo in Wei-hai-wei, at which time a coolie on board died of cholera. So when we arrived in Chefoo, the Japanese, having occupied Chefoo, put the ship under quarantine and would not allow us to even go ashore or to contact anybody except by radio. We were quarantined for approximately three weeks before the ship was allowed to proceed to Tientsin, where, upon arrival, the British were able to obtain our release from quarantine, and I proceeded by rail to Ch'in-huang-tao to rejoin the Bulmer.

Q: Did you find the Bulmer there?

Captain Kretz: Yes.

Q: Tell me, you spent three weeks on board this ship. Was it like being in prison?

Captain Kretz: No, in fact, it was very pleasant. We had good food, they had a nice bar, and the Japanese would come aboard every day and inspect us. We would mock them and make fun of them, and they'd get mad, but they couldn't do anything about it. They would come up with their white coats on and before they would leave the ship, they would put their feet up and have them sprayed, the soles of their feet sprayed and their garments sprayed.

Q: To kill the germs.

Captain Kretz: Kill the germs that they'd picked up on the ship before they left, so we would get in white coats and do it when they came in contact with us.

Q: You mimicked them.

Captain Kretz: Mimic them, yes.

Q: These were civil servants, I suppose? Japanese civil servants?

Captain Kretz: No, they were service people.

Q: And they didn't slap anybody. They just took it?

Captain Kretz: No, they just took it.

Q: That's interesting. When you joined the Bulmer, where did you go then?

Captain Kretz: We went down to South China and then to Olongapo.

Q: For overhaul, I suppose?

Captain Kretz: No, we were down there for operation and training.

Q: Gunnery, possibly. You returned to the States in a few months later, did you not?

Captain Kretz: Yes, a short time later. August, I guess, of '38.

Q: And how did you return?

Captain Kretz: We returned aboard the President Coolidge via Hong Kong and Yokohama, where I met my wife. She came over.

Kretz #2 - 80

Q: Any highlights on this cruise? The Coolidge was a new ship, wasn't it?

Captain Kretz: Not too new, no.

Q: It was a little fancier than the President Hayes?

Captain Kretz: Oh, yes, much fancier. It was a real nice ship, and we had very, very fine accommodations. It was a very, very pleasant cruise all the way back to the United States.

Q: Aboard the ship, were there many American wives and service dependents and so forth leaving the Orient because of the tense political situation?

Captain Kretz: There were several on board. In fact, most of them were Navy personnel, but they weren't leaving for that reason. They were leaving because their tours had expired and were going back to the States.

Q: I think it was in 1939 when they finally wouldn't let any more service wives go to the China station. In fact, they sent them home from there.

Captain Kretz: Yes, they did.

Kretz #2 - 81

Q: Do you have any particular lessons to pass on to young officers and their families if they go on detached duty?

Captain Kretz: You've got to take it as you find it.

Q: Well put!

Captain Kretz: And do the best you can, because you can't predict it. I'll give you one example here, if you want it.

Q: Fine.

Captain Kretz: In my whole naval career as a line officer, I had two collisions in which I was the officer of the deck. They both occurred on the same day. The first collision--they both were in the Bulmer--we left Shanghai and were on our way to Chefoo, and the Whangpoo River was just jam packed with sampans. One cut right directly in front of us. There was no missing it. Any way you turned, you were going to hit two or three. Well, we hit this sampan and cut it in two. We so informed the Commander in Chief Asiatic Fleet in the Augusta, and he told us to proceed on our duty as assigned, that they'd take care of it. The Chinese used to do that deliberately in order to sue the government and collect damages.

In the afternoon, I think I had the 12:00 to 4:00 watch.

Later I got off watch, and we had dinner, and Moe Vose had the second dog watch.* Moe had a terrific cold, so I told Moe, "Why don't you just turn in and then you won't have a watch 'til tomorrow afternoon. I'll take your second dog."

I went up on the bridge, and it was cold and foggy, very, very poor visibility. I remember we were making 12 knots, and as soon as I relieved the officer of the deck, I called down to the captain, and said that due to visibility conditions, I requested permission to slow to six knots. He said, "Permission not granted."

I said, "Also I have posted two new lookouts in the eyes." So I couldn't slow down. And just a few minutes later, a huge junk appeared in front of us, I think, about 7:30.

Q: How much visibility did you have ahead?

Captain Kretz: I would say we had 300 yards maximum. So the Chinese junk was ahead of us, and it was dark now. They hadn't had any lights on these Chinese junks. Sometimes they'd light a match if something was coming close, but they didn't do anything. I saw this thing appear ahead of us, so the first thing I did was grab the siren cord. Remember, you could reach right up and grab that thing. And I said, "Left, full rudder."

---

*Lieutenant (junior grade) James E. Vose, Jr., USN.

And I was just about to say, "Starboard engine ahead full," because we had the current of the river and we were a little to the left of this junk, and I wanted to get into this current and then swing around it.

The captain walked on the bridge, went over to the annunciators and said, "Back full" or "Stop," I've forgotten which.

Q: We're running out of time here and tape also. We'll carry on next week.

Interview Number 3 with Captain Charles Henry Kretz,
U.S. Navy (Retired)

Place: Captain Kretz's home in San Mateo, California

Date: 11 April 1984

Subject: U.S. Asiatic Fleet

Interviewer: Captain Paul B. Ryan, U.S. Navy (Retired)

Q: Captain Kretz, the last time, when we ended our last session, you were about to describe a collision with a Chinese junk that occurred when you were officer of the deck on the USS Bulmer, destroyer number 222. Do you want to pick up on that description from the beginning?

Captain Kretz: Yes. I took over the second dog watch, which is, of course, from 6:30 to 8:00 in the evening, on the third of May 1938. The ship was en route from Shanghai to Chefoo. We were going down the Yangtze River, and we were just turning north when I took over the deck. I immediately realized -- I saw that the ship had excessive speed. I think we were making 12 knots. I requested from the captain, over the intercom, to reduce the speed to six knots. I also informed the captain that I had put two new lookouts in the eyes of the ship because of the low visibility due to fog. A short time later, this huge junk appeared, I would say in the neighborhood of not more than 200 yards ahead of us. I immediately grabbed the siren cord and gave the order, "Left full rudder." My next order I intended to give was, "Starboard engine ahead full," to swing the ship, because we had to cut into the current of the Yangtze River to keep from being swept into this junk, even though we might possibly cross ahead of it without hitting it.

At that time, the captain came on the bridge.* He immediately grabbed the engine room annunciators to stop the engines and then ordered back two-thirds. At that, I realized we were going to collide with this junk because it stopped the swing of the ship, and we did collide with the junk.

The junk immediately started drifting away in the current. There were Chinese in the water, all screaming. We put a couple of boats over, tried to pick up the Chinese. They refused to get into our boats. We tried to follow the junk, to catch up with it, but it was drifting too fast and we were afraid we were going to lose our boats in the fog.

So we recalled our boats by searchlight. In the meantime, we had anchored. When we tried to get under way, the anchor refused to come up. The anchor engine would not budge it, so we put in the spokes in the capstan and manned the spokes, and finally we got the anchor up, but it was fouled in a cable, which later turned out to be the communication cable between China and Japan. In order to free the anchor, we cut this cable.

Q: What did you use, an acetylene torch?

---
*The commanding officer of the Bulmer was Lieutenant Commander Walter C. Ansel, USN.

Captain Kretz: No, we used fire axes.

Q: Chopped it up?

Captain Kretz: Chopped it up so we could get under way. We were going to try to find the junk, but we never did.

Q: So the junk was anchored but it lost its moorings and was swept down river.

Captain Kretz: It was being swept down river. I guess it was an ebb tide in the current.

Q: Did you see any Chinese in the river?

Captain Kretz: I didn't see any Chinese, but I heard them.

Q: Did you lower any boats to look for Chinese?

Captain Kretz: Yes, we lowered two boats, a pulling boat and a motor whaleboat--motor sampan, I guess we called it then. But we could not pick up any of the Chinese. They refused to get into our boats.

Q: Did anybody go aboard the junk?

Kretz #3 - 87

Captain Kretz: To my knowledge, nobody went aboard. We never did get actually to the junk.

Q: Did you get alongside?

Captain Kretz: As I remember, we did not get alongside the junk.

Q: So the captain came on the bridge without realizing that you had given orders to the rudder and to the engines. He went ahead and just gave his own orders without realizing the full import.

Captain Kretz: Well, no. He stated in his report that the first he knew that the collision was imminent was when he heard me give the order "Full left rudder." Well, I had never given that order in my life. My order was "left full rudder." At that time, I don't think that he had seen the junk.

Q: And he came on the bridge after you had sounded the signal?

Captain Kretz: After I sounded the siren. Apparently he was on his way up to the bridge when I sounded the siren.

Q: Well, the official report of this varies somewhat from your recollection, and he sent it in to the destroyer squadron commander.

Captain Kretz: Commander in Chief Asiatic Fleet.

Q: And nothing was heard from this?

Captain Kretz: I never heard anything back from it. Whether he received something back, I don't know.

Q: And no repercussions on cutting the cable?

Captain Kretz: No. We never reported the cutting of the cable.

Q: Captain, with your permission, I'll include a copy of the official report of this incident, which will become part of the oral history record.

Captain, one of the duties of the Yangtze Patrol gunboats was to provide armed guards to U.S. ships when they were steaming into a trouble situation. Did you ever have armed guard duty?

Captain Kretz: No, I never had armed guard duty. We were always prepared for any eventuality to happen, but just aboard ship. We didn't put any armed guard aboard any ship, and we didn't land any armed guards.

Q: You escorted merchant ships when needed?

Captain Kretz: Well, I don't ever remember actually escorting

Kretz #3 - 89

ships until after the Sino-Japanese War started, and then it was with destroyers.

Q: Did you have a landing force on the Panay, ready to go ashore any time? Could you have mustered a landing force?

Captain Kretz: We could have mustered a landing force, yes.

Q: And it was understood that if need be, you had to go.

Captain Kretz: We had to go, yes. But we never did.

Q: What about on board the Bulmer? Did you ever have occasion to have armed guard duty there?

Captain Kretz: Yes, I did. In October of 1937, we got word that the SS Steel Traveler, an American ship, was coming in to Shanghai.

Q: To Shanghai?

Captain Kretz: In to Shanghai. It was the first U.S. merchant ship to enter Shanghai since the start of the Sino-Japanese War. We received orders on the Bulmer to place an armed guard on board the Steel Traveler outside of the entrance to the Yangtze River. I was ordered to command of this armed guard.

Q: How many men were in the guard?

Captain Kretz: There were ten.

Q: Ten enlisted?

Captain Kretz: Ten enlisted. Yes, it was ten enlisted men and myself. We proceeded down the Whangpoo River in the <u>Bulmer</u> on the 29th of October and met the <u>Steel Traveler</u> at the mouth of the Yangtze River early on that same morning. We proceeded up the Yangtze River, then up the Whangpoo River to a British compound called the Pootung Wharf. We had no incidents on the way up. We had placed men with automatic rifles in strategic positions to help defend from any aircraft attacks or any boarding attacks, but we had no incidents until we arrived just off of the Pootung dock. A Japanese transport attempted to pass us to our starboard as we were pulling into dock at the wharf. At that time, two Chinese machine gun nests, one in front of us and one astern of us, opened up fire on this Japanese transport.

Q: That was anchored in the stream?

Captain Kretz: She was under way. She was pulling up to a dock on the other side of the river, on the west side of the river. Immediately the Japanese destroyers and cruisers in the area opened fire on this two machine gun nest, and six Japanese planes began strafing the area. The fire lasted for approximately one hour and then ceased. After the firing was over, I went ashore and went up to examine the machine gun nests to see just what was there, and it turned out that the Chinese had just been in the nests for a short period of time and opened up with a few blasts of their machine guns, and then ran back up trenches alongside the compound, which was a truncated shape. So the Japanese never did see them, and when the Japanese were doing all this firing at the machine gun nests, there was nobody in them.

Q: I see. But in the meantime, you and the Steel Traveler were exposed to all this fire.

Captain Kretz: Yes, we were in the middle.

Q: I see. But no one, fortunately, was hit, I gather.

Captain Kretz: Nobody was hit, no.

Q: Captain, you mentioned that you were armed with automatic rifles. Can you specify just what you did have?

Captain Kretz: Yes. Upon arrival aboard the Steel Traveler, the guard was stationed as follows. They had one Browning automatic rifle and assisted with service rifle in the bow, one Browning automatic rifle and assistant with service rifle on top of the after deck house, one signalman and assistant on the bridge. The remaining four riflemen were stationed amidships as lookouts and possibly airplane attack.

Q: How long did you stay on board?

Captain Kretz: I stayed on board until that afternoon at about 1:30, when I was relieved by a Marine detachment from the USS Augusta, the flagship of the Asiatic Fleet.

Q: When you say a service rifle, we're talking about the old Springfield 30-30?

Captain Kretz: Springfield 30-30, yes.

Q: Captain, I'd like to revert for a minute to your duty on board the Panay, which I can say right now was 191 feet long and had a draft of 5 feet 3 inches. You acted as navigator on board at one time, did you not?

Captain Kretz: The whole period. The whole year.

Q: What kind of navigation instruments did you use? I know you didn't use a sextant.

Captain Kretz: No, of course, we didn't use a sextant.* What we used were the buoys in the river and land markers.

Q: What about the magnetic compass?

Captain Kretz: Well, we didn't use the magnetic compass too much either. It was more by sight.

Q: Seaman's eye.

Captain Kretz: Seaman's eye. Always when we were moving up and down the river, we had a Chinese pilot on board. They knew that river like the back of their hand, and they could tell where the shallows were just by looking at it. And they could also tell where the currents were, so that we could be going up river and actually have a current pushing us.

Q: Did they speak much English?

Captain Kretz: A little. Enough to get by. But they also had their--I think we called them polemen, the Chinese.

Q: Do you want to describe their duties?

---
*The sextant is used for celestial navigation in the open ocean, out of sight of land.

Captain Kretz: They had bamboo poles. They were stationed, I think, two on each side. They would put the poles in the water as depth finders.

Q: So they took soundings, and the poles were marked off in feet, were they?

Captain Kretz: I don't remember whether it was feet or what it was, but they were marked so that they could tell.

Q: Were these 15-feet long poles or so?

Captain Kretz: About 15 feet long.

Q: How many did you have on board with the pilot?

Captain Kretz: We had four, as I remember, two on each side.

Q: Did these river buoys and markers ever get out of position?

Captain Kretz: I don't ever remember them being out of position.

Q: But the pilots would know if they had.

Captain Kretz: They would know, yes. But you've got to remember that that river, the contour of the channel was changing almost constantly, and the sandbars would fill up in a very short period of time. But the Chinese pilots were able to determine where they were, and we never went aground the whole time I was there.

Q: I understand that one of the tricks of the trade in the Yangtze River was to listen to your bow wave, and if it changed in character, the sound would tell you you were approaching a bad, shallow spot. Did you ever hear that?

Captain Kretz: I never heard that, no.

Q: Captain, the Chinese river charts that you used, where did you procure those?

Captain Kretz: As I remember, we got them from the Navy Purchasing Office in Shanghai; they kept us supplied.

Q: What did they look like? They weren't our conventional Hydrographic Office.

Captain Kretz: They weren't the Hydrographic Office charts. I don't remember too much what they did look like.

Q: Were they lithographs, blueprints?

Captain Kretz: I think they were blueprints, if I remember.

Q: Somebody must have been getting information from the Chinese pilots' association to keep them updated.

Captain Kretz: As I remember, the Chinese pilots had their own charts when they came aboard.

Q: Did they have a union of pilots?

Captain Kretz: Not that I knew of.

Q: Did they work for the Chinese Government or the Chinese Maritime Customs?

Captain Kretz: I don't remember who they worked for.

Q: Captain, one of the duties of a younger officer on board the Bulmer was that of commissary officer. Did you hold that job?

Captain Kretz: Yes, I did.

Q: What was the ration allowance for a U.S. sailor?

Captain Kretz: As I remember, it was 65 cents a day.

Q: Did your people eat well on that?

Captain Kretz: They ate very well. In fact, after I left and was detached from the Bulmer and was back in the United States, I received a letter from Scotty, a very close friend of mine who was back out in China and had been aboard the Bulmer. He went aboard the Bulmer to visit it, and all of the sailors wanted to know where I was. They said I had been the best commissary officer they had; they hadn't eaten so well since I left.

Q: And to what do you attribute that?

Captain Kretz: Well, watching what you buy and using what leftovers you could and then having real good meals when you could have them. One time--which I think contributed a lot to this--we were down off of Amoy and Foochow and we couldn't get provisions. We saved up all those rations, and we finally got into Hong Kong and splurged them all.

Q: You had steak every meal, that sort of thing?

Captain Kretz: Yes. We spent it all when we got to Hankow. That crew really ate for a while.

Q: Your ship was what they called a "good feeder" in those days.

Captain Kretz: Yes.

Q: Captain, one of the hazards of China duty was the fact that a lot of the vegetables and fruit that one bought in China were contaminated from the fertilizer and all that, the honey barges. How did you cope with this problem?

Captain Kretz: Well, as I remember, we parboiled just about everything that came aboard. That was the main thing that we did. We were very careful to be sure that everything was thoroughly washed. One of the big problems out there was ice.

Q: Contaminated ice.

Captain Kretz: Contaminated ice. I remember up in Chefoo where some children went into an ice cream freezer, you know, the crank type, and ate some of that ice.

Q: Chinese children?

Captain Kretz: No, some of our U.S. children. And they were very, very sick. I don't think that they died, but I think they got cholera. My wife, when we were in Shanghai, ate some strawberries one day and it turns out that they had not been parboiled. She contracted paratyphoid B and very nearly died. They thought we were going to lose her.

Q: Probably you could buy strawberries at the French Club and get this sort of thing, because I myself did.

Captain Kretz: Did you?

Q: I know what you're talking about.

Mrs. Kretz: We were at the Cathay Mansion when that happened.

Q: I see. So a reputable hotel restaurant.

Mrs. Kretz: Yes, very.

Q: So it was a dangerous life. Were there any medical problems for your doctor on board the Bulmer regarding diet?

Captain Kretz: Not that I remember. We didn't have a doctor aboard the Bulmer.

Q: You had a pharmacist's mate?

Captain Kretz: We had a pharmacist's mate and I'm not sure whether we had a doctor at that time or not. We had a pharmacist's mate, but I don't remember a doctor aboard the Bulmer. We had a doctor when we were tied up at the Texaco compound in Shanghai, and I think he was attached to the compound.

Kretz #3 - 100

Q: Your crew suffered no intestinal diseases?

Captain Kretz: Well, worms. Everybody had to be de-wormed.

Q: Where did they pick up these worms?

Captain Kretz: From food.

Q: Meat? Chicken?

Captain Kretz: Meat, chicken.

Mrs. Kretz: Hams, too.

Captain Kretz: Hams, yes.

Q: Did the Navy have a sure-fire method of curing worms?

Captain Kretz: Well, it sure got rid of everything you had in you.

Mrs. Kretz: Remember Cecil and the watermelon? My amah brought us a watermelon, and I was just delighted. I had a refrigerator. The doctor came up and said, "You'll have to throw that away."
   I said, "Oh, no."
   He said, "Yes, they take syringes and fill it with river

water and inject it into the watermelon to make it weigh more. They get a few more pennies, and you get dysentery."

Q: Captain, reverting back to the *Panay*, you were the communications officer. What type of codes did you carry on board?

Captain Kretz: We carried, as I remember, the strip code and we carried the cylinder code, which, as I remember it, was an aluminum thing. Maybe it was brass. But it was about 3 inches long or so with dials which could be turned. We had a key to set it up.

Q: There was a letter substitution code?

Captain Kretz: There was a letter substitution code.

Q: And the strip cipher was a series of thin strips inserted into a red leather folder, and that was again a letter substitution.

Captain Kretz: Same type of thing.

Q: There was another type of code in those days, five-letter group codes where you substituted words for five-letter groups.

Kretz #3 - 102

Captain Kretz: I don't remember that.

Q: But you had no secret coding machine?

Captain Kretz: No, we did not.

Q: But any traffic you sent, then, was in the strip cipher and the cylinder. Captain, I think it's true that the more technical a navy becomes, then the more the administration increases as far as paperwork goes, with forms to fill out and so forth. The Navy, after World War I, had become much more technologically advanced. Out there on the China Station, did you find yourself stifled in paperwork?

Captain Kretz: Yes, we did. Of course, we probably didn't have as much as we did in destroyers later on, but we still had plenty of paperwork. We would get all kinds of letters, "Why didn't you get this report in on time, or that report?" Or, "You made an error in this report," or something. We felt that we had much too much paperwork, and it wasn't accomplishing very much.

Q: Captain, is there any other episode that you recollect that we should include in your oral history?

Captain Kretz: Yes, I think of one that should be included. The _Bulmer_ went to North China, to Chefoo, in the late spring or early summer of 1938. As I have said before, my wife and I and our son lived in a cottage at the Strand Hotel in Chefoo the summer before. I'd like to describe the Strand Hotel. It consisted of a hotel building on the street with two rows of cottages stretching back from the hotel to the beach, with a courtyard in the center. The Japanese in command had taken over this hotel with their headquarters in the main hotel building and quartering their troops and officers in the cottages that we had lived in.

That evening, we invited the commanding officer of one of the Japanese destroyers over to dinner on the <u>Bulmer</u> and asked him to bring another couple of officers if he so desired. To our surprise, he accepted. He came over and brought one of his officers, and he also brought a young Japanese Navy lieutenant from the headquarters. Well, it turned out that this lieutenant had graduated from Princeton University in 1932, the same year that I graduated from the Naval Academy. He spoke perfect English, and we had quite an evening discussing the football games and things that happened during that fire fight on the beach during dinner time.

So he invited me over to his command the next day and said that he would send a car down to pick me up. Well, I went ashore the next afternoon, and he was at the dock to meet me with a staff car. There were a lot of rickshaws and rickshaw coolies there, and in fact, the one that we had hired for the summer when we were there before was there to pick me up. Of course, he had priority to pick me up against any of the others because he had worked for me. But he got awfully mad, and they all got mad, when I got in the staff car and wouldn't get in the rickshaw. We went up to the headquarters in the Strand Hotel and sat around and talked. He introduced me to several other Japanese officers. We had seaweed and saki, which was awful. Then he asked me if I would like to see some of the countryside and some of their installations. I said, "Certainly." I wanted to get all the information I could get.

So we left in the car, and we were going to go up to a tea house on the side of the mountain, where my wife and I used to go up sometimes in the evening and have tea and watch the sunset. It was a beautiful place.

On the way, we crossed a bridge. He said, "This is where all that shooting was last night that you heard on the ship." It was obvious they had quite a battle there. You could see the results of the battle.

So we went up to the tea house and had tea. He refused to pay; he just walked out. I slipped some money to the waitress. We went down and he said, "Would you like to go up in our trenches?"

So I said, "Yes," and he took me out to the front-line trench, and I had a Japanese soldier in front of me with a submachine gun and one in the back of me with a submachine gun. We toured through part of the trenches, then went back up to their headquarters.

After a little while, I said, "Well, I think I better be getting back to the ship."

He said, "Okay. I'll give you a staff car."

I said, "No, I've been at sea for a couple of months, and I think I'll walk off some of my sea legs. I'd just like to walk around Chefoo by myself."

He said, "Okay."

As I was walking down the street, I was looking to find some of the Chinese that I knew, some of these merchants that I had dealt with, to see if I could find out anything more that was going on in Chefoo. But all of their buildings were closed, the doors were locked, and the windows were all boarded up. Finally I came to a street corner and there were some Chinese children playing. As I passed, one of the little Chinese boys ran by me, and he kept telling me, "You follow me. You follow me. You follow me."

So I followed him, and he ran up the block a little ways, and then quickly turned in to an alley. I turned in to the alley, and just after I turned in the alley, a door opened, and here was one of the Chinese merchants. He pulled me in the door and closed the door. We went down through a lot of back alleys and corridors and so forth. Finally we arrived in a basement where there were several other Chinese merchants and a couple of Chinese Army officers. They told me right off the bat, they said, "You know what will happen if the Japanese catch us here. They'll do the same thing to you that they're going to do to us."

I said, yes, I realized that. He said, "Do you want to stay?"

I said, "Yes." So they gave me all the information they had on what the Japanese were doing, where they were, how many troops they thought they had, where the Chinese were. And then they led me back out and down a lot of back alleys and places I never knew existed in Chefoo, and we came out right down by the dock.

I went over, the boat was waiting for me, and I went over and got in the boat and went back in the ship.

Q: Did you then prepare a dispatch for commander in chief?

Captain Kretz: I prepared an intelligence report.

Q: Very valuable. Captain, after you were detached from the Bulmer in 1938, you were ordered back to the West Coast for duty. When you arrived, did you arrive in San Francisco?

Captain Kretz: Yes, we arrived in San Francisco on the President Coolidge.

Q: Did you experience some culture shock?

Captain Kretz: Well, the best thing we saw was when we saw the Golden Gate Bridge and went under it. It was being constructed when we left, and when we saw it, I guess it was completed at that time. Then we noticed that everybody seemed to be moving faster and rushing around more than we'd been used to in China and the Orient. We soon became accustomed to it and started doing the same thing.

Q: Where was your next posted duty?

Captain Kretz: Next, I was ordered to the Wasmuth when she was down in San Diego, another destroyer, four-stacker.

Q: Was this duty somewhat different from your China duty?

Captain Kretz: Well, it was entirely different in a way, and in other ways duty on a destroyer is duty on a destroyer.

Q: I'm talking about, I guess, your living in Coronado.

Captain Kretz: Yes, we lived in Coronado.

Q: Quite a difference from the Cathay Mansions.

Captain Kretz: Oh, yes.

Q: Captain, in concluding this series of very interesting interviews, if on your return to the West Coast in 1938, suppose a young ensign in 1938 had found out that you'd just returned from the China Station and he said to you, "Lieutenant, I just got my orders out to the Asiatic Fleet. Do you have any advice for me?" What would you have said to him?

Captain Kretz: Well, I would have advised him to request duty on the Yangtze River because it's something different from anything else that the Navy ever had or ever probably would have later, and something I think that he'd really enjoy. It was only a one-year tour at that time, just one year on the river, and then you were sent down to be in destroyers for another year and a half. At that time the tour was two and a half years. But I think you have experiences that you would never get any place else. There's no place in the world you could get the same experience. So I would advise him first to try to go on the Yangtze River and then destroyers in the Asiatic Fleet.

Q: I think it's fair to say that the Yangtze Patrol in 1938 was approaching the end of an era in naval history.

Captain Kretz: Yes, but we didn't realize that too much. We knew that--at least I was positive in my own mind that within just a few years we were going to be at war with Japan, and I so expressed that many times in many places.

Q: I think you're fortunate, you and Mrs. Kretz both, to have had this unique experience, and thank you very much for this fascinating account.

Captain Kretz: Thank you. I hope I've given you some information that might be of value to somebody some day.

Q: I'm sure you have.

Retyped Copy of Letter Dated 3 May 1938

A4-3/H3(196)

                                              Enroute Shanghai to Chefoo,
                                                3 May 1938.

From: Commanding Officer.
To: Commander in Chief, Asiatic Fleet.

Subject: Low Visibility Contact with Chinese Fishing
              Junk Off Yangtze Entrance 3 May, 1938.

    1. The U.S.S. Bulmer collided with an anchored Chinese fishing junk off the Yangtze entrance in low visibility on the evening of 3 May, 1938, while enroute Shanghai to Chefoo, China. A six by six foot section of the junk's starboard bow was stove in above the water line; no damage was suffered by the Bulmer. Attending circumstances and further details are given in the paragraphs below.

    2. The Bulmer having cleared the Yangtze Light Vessel on course 090° had just reduced speed to 10 knots because of fog when the shape of a vessel was sighted about 10 degrees on the starboard bow. The Commanding Officer's attention was directed to it by the Officer-of-the-Deck's order of full left rudder. The shape appeared to be a fishing junk, distant about 5 to 7 hundred yards; there appeared to be plenty of room and time to clear it to the left, which was the direction toward which the ship was already swinging. However, because of the known undependability of the maneuvering of junks, the Commanding Officer ordered the engines stopped and then backed two-thirds.

    3. Backing the engines checked the ship's swing and it was realized that the ship was being swept on the junk by the strong tide setting to the right (180°). The junk was seen to be anchored; no one was visible and no signals were being made. The engines were therefore put ahead again at two-thirds in an effort to snake the ship around the junk's bow. She was headed about 340°. The wind force 2, was from the Southeast, sea calm.

    4. The Bulmer's bow cleared but the starboard side at the bridge took the junk in the bow, broke her from her morrings and crushed in a section about 6 feet square around the starboard eye.

A4-3/H3/(196)

Subject: Low Visibility Contact With Chinese Fishing
          Junk Off Yangtze Entrance 3 May, 1938.

---

5. At the shock of contact Chinamen tumbled up aft in the junk and commenced shouting. The ship was backed down and anchored with the junk abeam. It was thought at the time that the junk would be in danger of sinking and that her men would be in the water. Under the visibility prevailing and night falling it was desired to definitely fix the position for further action.

6. The pulling whaleboat with the Executive Officer in charge, followed by the motor whaleboat with the Engineer Officer, proceeded to the junk. The motor whaleboat in a short time reported that the junk was in no danger, that a small section had been broken from her starboard bow and that her crew was uninjured and all accounted for. The motor whaleboat then returned to the junk, now out of sight and rapidly drifting to leeward. The Executive Officer and Engineer Officer examined it further and then returned to the ship. They reported that the junk was compartmented and athwartships into about 6 compartments. All were dry, including the injured foremost one, which is usually kept open and used for net stowage. A section that included the conventional junk eye on the starboard bow had been broken off down to a point about 1-1/2 to 2 feet above the water line. The broken section had been recovered and was secured by a line. The anchor line had been parted but a spare anchor was available. The Chinese fishermen, of which there were eight, at first were not badly perturbed; they exhibited their fish, and their poor clothing, apparently in an effort to convince the officers of the honesty of their occupation. Space was offered in the ship's boats, even to pushing them and motioning to them in but they refused to leave their craft; they also refused money proffered to pay for repairs. Later it was realized that the fishermen probably thought themselves under suspicion of smuggling or blockade breaking and that they really feared military action of some sort. When no progress could be made with the Chinese fishermen, life jackets were left on the junk and the boats returned to report at the ship.

7. It was decided to hoist boats and anchor, proceed alongside the junk and attempt to effect repairs or help in any other possible way. The anchor came up fouled with a cable and 25 minutes were consumed in clearing it. The ship then steamed

A4-3/H3/(196)

Subject: Low Visibility Contact With Chinese Fishing
          Junk off Yangtze Entrance 3 May, 1938.

---

slowly in the direction of the current (170°) toward the supposed location of the junk. Searchlights were used on either bow but the heavy fog still prevailed and very little could be seen. The search was continued on various courses for about an hour without success.

    8. The situation was then thoroughly reviewed and carefully reconsidered with the following results:

      (a) that there was little chance of finding the junk.

      (b) that it was doubtful that anything could be done for it if found;
      (c) that the junk was in no real danger;
      (d) that under the existing situation of fog, strong currents, proximity of shoals (latitude 30°56', longitude 122°33' E) and traffic lane, the Bulmer might be in danger.

It was therefore decided to clear the area and proceed on assigned duty.

                                            WALTER ANSEL.

Copy to:
      Comdesron Five;
      Comdesdiv Fourteen.

Index

to

Reminiscences of

Captain Charles Henry Kretz, Jr.

Supply Corps, U.S. Navy (Retired)

U.S. Naval Institute

Annapolis, Maryland

1986

Amoy, China
  USS Bulmer (DD-222) was close to the fighting between Japanese and the Chinese in 1937, page 66

Ansel, Lieutenant Commander Walter C., USN (USNA, 1919)
  Commanding officer of the Bulmer (DD-222) when the destroyer suffered two collisions on the Yangtze River on 3 May 1938, pages 81-85, 87
  Report on collisions, See Appendix

Arkansas, USS (BB-33)
  Embarked contingent of Marines in anticipation of taking them to Korea in 1932, page 1; midshipman cruise to Hawaii in 1933, pages 1-2

Armed Guard
  Bulmer (DD-222) provided guard for first merchant ship to enter Shanghai after outbreak of Sino-Japanese War in October 1937, pages 89-92

Army-Navy Football Game
  Officers listen to 1936 game via radio on China Station, page 46

Asiatic Fleet, U.S.
  Operations of the gunboat Panay (PR-5) on China's Yangtze River in 1936-37, pages 2, 12-24, 26-29, 33-34, 41, 101-102; administrative matters in late 1930s handled by Navy Purchasing Office in Shanghai, pages 5-6; operations of the destroyer Bulmer (DD-222) in China in 1937-38, during the Sino-Japanese War, pages 48-103; fleet commander in chief, Admiral Harry Yarnell, requested more ships from the Chief of Naval Operations in 1937, pages 62-63; Kretz's reflections on the unusual nature of duty on the China Station in the mid-1930s, pages 107-108

Atrocities
  By the Japanese in 1937 during the Sino-Japanese War, pages 51-53, 60-62

Britain
  See Royal Navy

Bulmer, USS (DD-222)
  First U.S. warship sent to Shanghai after 1937 Japanese attack, pages 48-49; guarded Texaco compound on Whangpoo River, pages 50-52, 56, 61, 70, 99; trained torpedoes at Japanese ships after Panay sunk in December 1937, pages

63-64; established communications with Americans in Tsingtao during Japanese invasion in 1937, pages 64-65; Japanese menaced Bulmer with shells at Amoy, page 66; officers in late 1930s, page 67; Kretz's duties as commissary officer, pages 68-69, 71-72, 96-101; maintenance and repairs done at small shipyard on Whangpoo River, pages 72-74; training off Olongapo, page 79; collided with two Chinese vessels in one day while Kretz was officer of the deck in May 1938, pages 81-88, appendix; armed guard mustered when merchant ship Steel Traveler entered Shanghai in October 1937, pages 89-92; medical services aboard, pages 99-100; administrative work, page 102; hosted Japanese officers in Chefoo in 1938, page 103

Canopus, USS (AS-9)
Evacuated U.S. dependents from Chefoo during Sino-Japanese War in 1937, pages 55-57

Chefoo, China
Site of intriguing encounter between Kretz and Japanese naval officer in the summer of 1938, pages 102-106

Chiang Kai-shek
Popularity with the Chinese people in the mid-1930s, page 24

China
Living accommodations in the mid-1930s, pages 6, 10-11, 44; help for Navy dependents, pages 6, 8, 43; burial practices in the 1930s, pages 9, 38-40; Chinese mess boys in U.S. ships in the mid-1930s, page 16; examples of the poor quality of cooperation afforded the Navy by the U.S. Embassy staff in the mid-1930s, pages 24-30, 52-53; American missionaries stationed in China in the mid-1930s came under the protection of the U.S. Asiatic Fleet, pages 14, 30-33; breakdown of population of I-ch'ang, page 33; examples of cheapness of life in the 1930s, pages 40-41; medical services for foreigners, page 43; lawlessness and security, pages 44-45; massacre by Japanese of civilians during Sino-Japanese War, pages 51-53; U.S. seemed indifferent to China's plight until Panay (PR-5) sunk in 1937, page 63; Bulmer (DD-222) established contact with Americans in Tsingtao during Japanese invasion in 1937, pages 64-65; U.S. ships repaired in Chinese shipyards, pages 72-74; Chinese pilots and polemen used in Panay (PR-5), pages 93-95; Chinese river charts provided by Navy purchasing office in Shanghai, pages 95-96; description of

Strand Hotel in Chefoo from 1938 when Japanese occupied it, pages 103-104; Kretz prepared intelligence report at Chefoo in 1938 based on his tour by a Japanese officer and Chinese hidden away after the Chefoo assault, pages 103-106

Cholera
When coolie on Chinese passenger ship died of cholera in 1938, the Japanese quarantined the ship at Chefoo, pages 77-79; U.S. children at Chefoo contracted Cholera after eating contaminated ice cream, page 98

Codes
Casual attitude toward codes by U.S. embassy personnel in China in the mid-1930s, pages 27-30; types of codes used by Panay (PR-5) in mid-1930s in China, pages 101-102

Collisions
Bulmer (DD-222) collided with two Chinese vessels in one day on the Yangtze River in May 1938, pages 81-88, appendix

Commissary Duty
As Bulmer (DD-222) commissary officer in 1937-1938, Kretz negotiated with wily Chinese merchants, pages 68-69, 71-72; allowance per sailor, page 96; Kretz's success in this duty, page 97

Communications
Native communications through China in 1930s, pages 8-9, 42; embassy communications handled through station ship at Nanking in the 1930s, pages 27-30; Bulmer established contact with Americans in Tsingtao during Japanese invasion in 1937, pages 64-65; codes in Panay (PR-5) in the mid-1930s, pages 101-102

Ekvall, Lieutenant (junior grade) Leslie D., MC, USN
Panay (PR-5) doctor treated officers after hunting trips in the mid-1930s, pages 36-38

Enlisted Personnel
Enlisted crew members of the gunboat Panay (PR-5) had Chinese servants to help with their work in the mid-1930s, pages 16-17; limited liberty opportunities for Panay crew in I-ch'ang, China, pages 33-34

Food
Officers from the gunboat Panay (PR-5) bagged ducks and

pheasants in China for the wardroom mess in the mid-1930s, pages 36-39; as commissary officer in Bulmer (DD-222) in the late 1930s, Kretz negotiated with wily Chinese merchants to obtain provisions for the Asiatic Fleet, pages 68-69, 71-72; special precautions taken with food in China, pages 98-101

Ford, Lieutenant Robert S., USN (USNA, 1927)
Served as witness when Kretz put the skipper of the Panay (PR-5) on report in the late 1930s, page 21; listened to 1936 Army-Navy football game on the radio while serving on China Station, page 46; Mrs. Ford met Mrs. Kretz in Manila after she was evacuated during the Sino-Japanese War, page 58

Great Britain
See Royal Navy

Guns
Arms used by Bulmer (DD-222) armed guard escorting Steel Traveler to Shanghai in October 1937, pages 91-92

Holton, Lieutenant Commander Chester M., USN (USNA, 1917)
Considered eccentric as Panay (PR-5) skipper in mid-1930s, page 17; anecdote about Holton and wife feeding birds on Panay, pages 18-19; dispute with the Panay's executive officer, pages 20-21; removed as commanding officer after Kretz wrote to CinC Asiatic Fleet about conditions on the ship, pages 21-23; hospitalized for mental problems, page 23

Hunting
Pheasant and duck hunting were popular pastimes for Yangtze River Patrol personnel in the mid-1930s, pages 36-39

I-ch'ang, China
Base for U.S. gunboat Panay (PR-5) in mid-1930s, pages 2, 33-34; accommodations ashore for the Kretzes in 1936, pages 11-12

Intelligence
Kretz filed a report on Chiang Kai-shek's reception in Nanking, China, following his release by the Communists in the mid-1930s, page 24; Kretz submitted a report at Chefoo, China, in 1938, based on a tour with a Japanese officer and visit with Chinese, pages 103-106

Japan
   Invasion of Shanghai in July 1937, pages 48-49; effort to retain neutrality by U.S. ships in China in 1937, pages 50-51; carried U.S. mail to China in the mid-1930s and censored it, page 52; quarantined passenger ship at Chefoo in 1938 when a coolie died of cholera, pages 77-79; Japanese officer showed Kretz gun sites at Chefoo in 1938, pages 103-105

Kretz, Audrey Raymer
   Accompanied husband to China via President Hayes in 1936, pages 2-3; accustomed to life in China, pages 8, 12; trip up Yangtze in Wulin in 1936, pages 9-10, 39-40; children, pages 41-43; evacuated to Philippines during Sino-Japanese War, pages 55-60; returned to China in 1938, pages 75-76; health, pages 76-77, 98

Kretz, Captain Charles Jr., USN   (USNA, 1932)
   Service in Arkansas (BB-33), 1932-1934, pages 1-2; family, pages 2-3, 8-10, 12, 39, 41-43, 55-60, 70, 75, 98, 103; communications and intelligence officer and assistant first lieutenant in Panay (PR-5), 1936-1937, pages 2-47, 92-96, 101-102; duty in Bulmer (DD-222) (1937-1938), pages 48-92, 96-106; duty in Wasmuth (DD-338) in 1938, page 107

Liberty
   For U.S. Navy personnel in China in the 1930s, pages 34, 36

Liquor
   Wine mess in Royal Navy ships in China in the late 1930s enjoyed by U.S. naval officers, pages 70-71

Marines, U.S.
   Temporarily embarked in Arkansas (BB-33) in the early 1930s in anticipation of service in Korea, page 1; in Shanghai in 1937 after outbreak of Sino-Japanese War, pages 53-54

Medical Services
   Panay (PR-5) doctor treated officers after hunting trips along the Yangtze River in the mid-1930s, pages 36-38; Bulmer (DD-222) pharmacist's mate treated crew for worms, pages 99-100

Missionaries
   One of Yangtze River Patrol's purposes in mid-1930s was to protect missionaries, page 14; in general, not

particularly cooperative with Navy in China, pages 30-31; vacationed in Chefoo, page 32; mission in China, page 33

Murfin, Admiral Orin G., USN (USNA, 1897)
Commander in Chief Asiatic Fleet takes his family up the Yangtze in the mid-1930s, pages 11-12

Nanking, China
Chiang Kai-shek welcomed to this Chinese capital after release by the Communists in the late 1930s, page 24; frustrations of trying to plan for possible evacuation of American embassy personnel in the late 1930s, pages 25-26; U.S. Navy station ship at Nanking provided communications link for U.S. embassy in the late 1930s, pages 27-30; explosion of gasoline demonstrated cheapness of life in China in mid-1930s, page 41

Navigation
Yangtze River piloted by the Panay (PR-5) in the 1930s, pages 92-93

Panay, USS (PR-5)
Kretz joined ship at I-ch'ang in 1936, pages 2, 5, 12; crew in the mid-1930s, pages 13, 17; trip from I-ch'ang to Shanghai, pages 13-14; fight with Chinese pirates, page 14; armament, pages 15, 26; accommodations aboard, page 16; Chinese mess boys, page 16; commanded by eccentric skipper, Lieutenant Commander Chester M. Holton, in late 1930s, pages 17-23; morale, pages 17, 19; officers hunted ducks and pheasant, pages 36-39; sinking in December 1937 brought U.S. attention to situation in China, pages 63-64, 67; navigation instruments aboard, pages 92-93; Chinese pilots and polemen used, pages 93-95; codes used by ship in the mid-1930s, pages 101-102

Pay and Allowances
Junior officer salary in China in the mid-1930s, pages 7-8

Philippines
Navy families evacuated from China to Baguio during the Sino-Japanese War, pages 56-60, 75-76; description of Baguio in the late 1930s, pages 59-60; major repairs on ships in the Far East done at Cavite in the late 1930s, page 74

President Coolidge, SS
Kretzes returned to United States from China in this passenger ship in 1938, pages 75-76, 79, 106

President Hayes, SS
　　Enjoyable ride to China for Kretzes on board this passenger liner in 1936, pages 2-5

Proteus, HMS
　　Kretz enjoyed wine mess during visit to this British submarine in China in the late 1930s, pages 70-71

Repairs and Maintenance
　　Upkeep of U.S. Navy vessels in China in the late 1930s performed at Chinese shipyards, pages 72-74

River Charts
　　Chinese charts provided to U.S. ships by Navy purchasing office in Shanghai, pages 95-96

Roblin, Lieutenant (junior grade) Robert D., Jr., USN (USNA, 1932)
　　Kretz's U.S. Naval Academy roommate relieved him at Tsingtao in 1937, page 65

Royal Navy
　　In China during Sino-Japanese War, page 62; liquor aboard ships in China enjoyed by U.S. guests, pages 70-71; fraternization between U.S. and British sailors in China in the late 1930s, page 71

San Francisco, California
　　Kretz's impressions of city in 1938 after two years in the Orient, pages 106-107

Shanghai, China
　　Navy purchasing office at Shanghai handled many administrative matters for the U.S. Asiatic Fleet in the late 1930s, pages 5-6; living conditions for Navy wives ashore, pages 6-8; site of fighting between Japanese and Chinese in war which began in 1937, pages 47-51, 54-56; Chinese were victims of Japanese atrocities in 1937, pages 61-62; Mrs. Kretz infected with paratyphoid in Shanghai from eating contaminated food, pages 76-77, 98-99; crew of USS Bulmer (DD-222) provided armed guard for U.S. merchant ship Steel Traveler at Shanghai in October 1937, pages 89-92

Sino-Japanese War
　　Bulmer (DD-222) first U.S. warship sent to Shanghai after July 1937 invasion by the Japanese, pages 48-50; atrocities by Japanese, pages 51-53, 60-62; U.S. Marines sent in, pages 53-54; U.S. dependents evacuated, pages 55-56; Bulmer (DD-222)

armed guard exposed to heavy fire while escorting merchant ship to Shanghai in October 1937, pages 89-92

Standard Oil Company
Presence in China in the mid-1930s, pages 4, 11, 15

Steel Traveler, M/V
Steel Traveler was provided an armed guard by Bulmer (DD-222) in October 1937 when it was the first merchant ship to enter Shanghai after the start of the Sino-Japanese War, pages 89-92

Steinbauer, Lieutenant Frederick S., USN   (USNA, 1921B)
Panay (PR-5) executive officer arrived in China via President Hayes in 1936, pages 4-5; poor relationship with Panay skipper, pages 19-21; tried to find Mrs. Kretz a place to stay in the Philippines after she evacuated from Chefoo, pages 57-58

Texaco
Bulmer (DD-222) protected the Texaco compound on the Whangpoo River in 1937, pages 50-52, 56, 61, 70, 99

Torpedoes
Destroyer Bulmer (DD-222) trained torpedo tubes at nearby Japanese warships at Tsingtao, China, after the sinking of the USS Panay (PR-5) in 1937, pages 63-64

Tsingtao, China
Activities of the destroyer Bulmer (DD-222) and her crew in this port after the sinking of the USS Panay (PR-5) at Nanking in 1937, pages 63-66; site of minor overhaul for the USS Bulmer (DD-222) in 1937, page 73

Vose, Lieutenant (junior grade) James E., Jr., USN   (USNA, 1934)
Kretz took fellow Bulmer (DD-222) officer Vose's watch as officer of the deck in May 1938, and the ship experienced her second collision of the day, page 82

Wulin, SS
British river steamer which took the Kretzes up the Yangtze River in the mid-1930s, pages 9, 12, 13, 40, 39

Yangtze River Patrol
Kretz's recollections of first trip up Yangtze River in mid-1930s, pages 8-10, 39-40; mission of patrol in mid-1930s, pages 14-15; opportunities for sailors on liberty, page 34; length of service for enlisted personnel on China Station, pages 34-35; collision between Bulmer and Chinese merchant vessels in May 1938, pages 81-88, appendix; Bulmer (DD-222) provided armed

guard for merchant ship entering Shanghai in October 1937, pages 89-91; Chinese pilots did skilled job of conning vessels on the Yangtze, pages 93-95; Kretz considers Yangtze patrol duty as one of the most interesting tours in the Navy, page 108
See also USS Panay (PR-5)

Yarnell, Admiral Harry E., USN (USNA, 1897)
Commander in Chief Asiatic Fleet in the late 1930s requested more ships be sent to his command, but was turned down, pages 62-63; tolerant of modified routine employed by ships in China, page 74

www.ingramcontent.com/pod-product-compliance
Lightning Source LLC
Chambersburg PA
CBHW080611170426
43209CB00007B/1397